REVERSE RAPTURE

Books by Dara Wier

Reverse Rapture
Hat on a Pond
Voyages in English
Our Master Plan
Blue for the Plough
The Book of Knowledge
All You Have in Common
The 8-Step Grapevine
Blood, Hook & Eye

Limited Editions

Fly on the Wall
(X in Fix)

VERSE PRESS (AMHERST, MA)

REVERSE RAPTURE

DARA WIER

Published by Verse Press

Library of Congress Cataloging-in-Publication Data

Wier, Dara
  Reverse rapture / Dara Wier.-- 1st ed.
    p. cm.
  ISBN 0-9746353-4-0 (alk. paper)
  I. Title.
  PS3573.I357R48 2005
  811'.54--dc22

    2004027071

Verse Press titles are distributed to the trade by Consortium Book Sales
and Distribution, 1045 Westgate Drive, St. Paul, MN 55114.

Cover Art by Metka Krasovec
Front Cover: Room (Door, Table, Chair)
Back Cover: Silence (Small Coat)
Used by permission of the artist.

Book designed and composed by J. Johnson.
Text set in Electra. Display set in Trade Gothic.
Printed in Canada

9 8 7 6 5 4 3 2 1

First Edition

for Emily
for Guy
for Jim

and in memory of
Euphrasie Zeolide Barrois
Gerard Hypolyte Barrois

Contents

Prologue

a stick, a cup, a bowl, a comb

These were some of their laws:

These were a few of the miles they cruised:

Here is where their beds went down:

With this their fate was sealed:

These are some things they shared:

These were with what they were comforted:

In this manner were they made to be cared for:

In these ways were they shaped to be seen:

Among these things were what they could bear:

In this time here is what they will be shown:

With this will they be remembered:

These were some of their customs:

These were with what they kept to themselves:

Here is a place they questioned:

In this way were they asked to provide:

There were what they provided:

In these instances thus were they praised:

It was with this were they wondering:

These were with what they marked themselves:

With this will they be never forgotten:

These were some of their means:

Here is an example of one of their methods:

With this did they solace themselves:

With this did they adorn themselves:

In these ways did they keep their provisions:

This is what they did with what they were fond of:

By this practice did they shore up magnificence:

These were what they were asked to furnish:

They caused these things to be memorized:

These were their most common rituals:

Among these these were considered unnecessary:

And in these were they in surplus:

These things they misused:

And prized:

And forfeited:

And pitied:

By these means did they resist their discovery:

These were some of the choices they made:

With these did they choose to be represented:

With these did they divine:

And with this were they occupied:

With these things did they labor:

For these things did they hope:

For these did they say they would die for:

These were the bargains they struck:

This is what they were given in exchange:

This is how they recognized one another:

By these means was love aroused:

Here are fragments of what they worshipped:

Among these things they passed their days:

Here is what they were willing to sacrifice:

In the traces of these things they were known by:

This is what they have left:

Here is where they left without a trace:

These were some of their gifts:

called back

(and then it moves back in at the end of the day)
(they're sundogs) (there's no way to catch one)
(you don't do anything, you try to look like a
rubberneck) (you try not to put a horse there)
(those are pronghorns) (why can't they be ante-
lopes) (we were walking inside a duststorm)
(you were born in a duststorm) (you say so as if
it means something) (it blew in some magpies)
(it came in under the doorframes) (we were migrating)

(you rolled up the blueprints) (you rolled up the
sidewalks) (it's a gametrail) (like biofeedback)
(it looks as if it used to be somebody's backyard)
(it's covered with lawnmowers) (that's a solution)
(like bentwood) (like an arroyo) (after a flash
flood) (that's where we went to find arrowheads)
(it was a reflex) (as if someone had hammered its
kneecaps) (they were always saying they weren't
saying what they were saying) (it made it hard to

follow them) (they were telling us they had to make
up their own minds) (it looked like an enclave)
(it wasn't a sewing bee) (they said we'd just have
to believe whatever it was they wanted us to)
(it looks as if it used to be a ballfield) (all
that's left is a little slice of rubber)
(it was a slider) (that's a place to put the side
lines) (that's a line drawn in a basin of water)
(we needed a better light source) (we needed

sugarcane) (we needed our caneknives) (we needed
dry blankets) (we couldn't get away from the under-
currents) (they were everywhere) (they were thick
as thieves) (they never seemed to mind that) (you
said they are what they are) (like a tarpatch)
(it sounded as if someone were cranking in a really
old fishing line) (but it was amplified) (like it
was pre-historic) (it was their paydirt) (they
wanted to put it in vending machines) (we would

be paying for it with our shirts) (and with our
pith) (that's what happens to cattle) (they call
it a necklace for short) (what if you resist be-
lieving that) (they'll say you're an ephebe)
(they'll say you reek of colostrum) (like jaw-
breakers) (like see-saws) (you'll be booby-
trapped) (you'll wish we were sunspots) (that's
how we got here) (it was written all over the
asphalt) (we needed someone to translate)

(something that was necessary) (not because they
had nothing to say) (or maybe they were afraid to
say it) (maybe they were afraid it would be too
costly) (I doubt it) (it seemed to be antiseptic)
(too antiseptic, it killed everything) (that is
an exaggeration) (it was a flare up) (it was a
flame-thrower's decoy) (it's written all over a
wristband) (you came in bobbing around) (you called
it dancing) (you ricocheted because you had to)

(there was still dew on the grass) (you were
frisky) (if you want to call it that) (everyone
was frisking everybody) (they said it felt good)
(they were practicing a new kind of hero-worship)
(it was deep-fried) (we needed to be decapods)
(we were supposed to roll with the punches) (as
though we were boiling) (as though we needed to
be) (so say you're some kind of star) (become
angry) (don't let them take your picture) (be

sullen) (feel as if no one understands you)
(it looked as if it were some kind of dealership)
(so we deviated) (we variegated) (you were the
marshal of that parade) (we took over a convent)
(we didn't stencil) (we were rifle birds) (you
said we were ordinary people) (we didn't like fly-
paper) (we had a few yardsticks) (we needed to
reconnoiter) (you were the one who could go in
and out of the house without notice) (you were

noiseless) (you were never baptized) (there were
several other options) (we needed to spend a
night in a cypress grove) (like bloodhounds)
(you were self-propelled) (like a distributary)
(when a thought flickered over your face)
(when you ran a hand through your hair)
(when headlights crossed over your cheekbones)
(when you shifted away to look into something)
(you were the one with oars in your hands)

domain of a hidden evening

(overtaken by night) (is all that happened) (just as
it did every evening) (as in those belated obsolete
times) (that was when a mouse slinked down the shadows
alongside a wall to its tiny little rooms to obsess
every night over its fear of growing larger) (there
are worse phobias) (fears of going to bed at night)
(of ice and music and birds and flutes and money)
(fear of swallowing) (of being wrong) (fear of not)
(understanding) (of missing out on something)

(whenever a certain one said *aggravation*) (it was
hard not to be put in mind of an auger) (in a gravel
pit) (with a mind of its own) (hard at work grinding)
(up all the words in the world) (and not of one small
pebble in the heel of a sock) (I remembered when
it became clear) (that sounding like a broken record)
(didn't mean I'd done something) (really very exciting)
(and it sounded like some kind of mania) (like the one
about the 2nd Coming of Christ) (or joy in complaining)

(remember how it used to be possible) (to make every
singer sound like a mouse) (by adjusting the speed of
a turntable) (that was aggravating) (and is obsolete)
(and who do we have to thank) (if words are shadows
as some say they are) (and they do not look like shadows)
(while they lie on a page) (what is the light that)
(doesn't pass through) (invisible things) (these words
must be) (or something like that) (I overheard last night)
(it's probably ambergris) (or isinglass) (or lacecloth)

(it feels pretty good to shimmy) (but it can look
like a frenzy) (now I find out just a little too late
phrenology's the science of teaching men how to
phrenologize without their knowing) (to size up
their inclinations and measure their vanities) (or
lusts) (or compassions or cares) (or obsessions or fears)
(sooner or later the mouse is going to miche back
out of its house) (and perhaps lavish in the fields)
(it was semi-private) (semi-peaceful) (semi-romantic)

(it was almost impossible) (not to start misdemeaning)
(once we got to the mezzanine) (overtaken by night)
(where so many mind-readers were milling around) (it
was all one could do) (not to perish the thought) (to
profess one knows someone else's thoughts) (some-
one's semi-private thoughts) (I guess, is so out-
landish) (it's understandable it would be fashionable)
(too much overbrowsing was driving all of the second-
guessing farther) (and farther) (into the wilderness)

(a fellow told me this morning) (some bears are so shy)
(they walk backwards) (to avoid meeting people) (they
walk backwards in their own tracks to go where they
want to get) (and that's understandable though it
seems it would be overaggravating) (to any reasonable
bear) (a rock jockey told me there's a bear in her
woods who likes to come up to the house and stare)
(through her windows) (it's another way they have
of turning the tables) (and a curious look is charming)

(as is a look of candor) (and a camelhair jacket)
(an ex-fisherman I know who's become a weaver
and is a keeper of camels says once a camel gets
to know you it will remember you forever) (and
it will know everything there is to know about
your character) (so be careful) (so be careless)
(or cautious) (or mutinous or mountainous) (but don't
be a miser) (fear of money is what that amounts to)
(whatnot to fear that) (there is nothing to fear)

(overtaken by night) (just a little belated) (one
hopes there will still be room) (at the table)
(I'm thinking of the table with these thoughts
on it) (layers of candlewax and fallen
petals) (a moose with a broken antler) (a worn out
elf with a curious look on its face) (a girl pre-
tending she's reading a book) (a brave-looking goat)
(who's waiting to have its legs delivered) (a tiny
skull with its regions marked off) (a monkey on

wheels) (three gold mice as small as grains of rice)
(eating poppyseeds) (a pair of farmers in their go-to-
town clothes) (sitting in a field) (a red-winged blackbird)
(a pelican) (a condor) (a finch) (a fork someone's bent)
(a bowl someone's used) (a stack of news of the day and
yesterday and the day before) (that and the day before
that) (if you think when I'm reading I'm reading) (to send
what I'm thinking) (along for the ride) (you're right about
that) (like a pebble in the auger of its mania)

So.

(for a while) (we lived in a house with bars on
its windows)
(there was an evil genius) (concocting a cubist music)
(to frighten the children with)
(to find the ammunition dump you take Animal Road)
(you put on a dress, you put on a scarf)
(it's a little past the radio station but you can't
see it) (it's been burned down)
(we can make a raft of the bedframes) (we can turn

the curtains into sails) (we'll find something to
row with) (nothing can be motorized)
(we hadn't been cursed or blessed) (we'd been syncopated)
(so we didn't talk like we used to) (we didn't walk like
we used to) (we made up new ways to walk) (to many of the
same places) (but we didn't see the same things there)
(as we used to see)
(though it didn't seem as if it made any sense) (to force
how we were feeling) (to be synchronized)

(there was no convincing evidence to feel otherwise)
(it was still the habit in those days to apply) (the
ancient three-ply solution to everything) (like clockwork)
(with a metronomical insistent amnesia clause inside)
(some things were taking a clobbering)
(some things weren't in the position to synthesize)
(even when I suspended some pretty cisele chiseled with
night jasmine over some of the windows I froze)
(where do you get 'em) (you get 'em at the landfill)

(it's open a couple of hours every other Sunday)
(but it's closed)
(look how they've spruced up the thought trans-
ference booths) (that's an institutional green
to die for) (if I ever saw one)
(once I went with two strangers) (who were out) (chasing
tornadoes) (once was enough of that) (once when a
tornado was chasing me I took refuge) (in a drugstore)
(the druggist always sent me away with a little tin

of something) (something he'd concocted with a mortar
& a pestle) (he liked me) (I was a mobile addition
to his honky tonk laboratory) (and he admired my
calciform nose)
(every shredder served a different purpose)
(the one for false pretenses was way undersized) (or
undersiege or underutilized) (it was fatigued)
(you look for your shoes) (you don't need your keys)
(you put the travois where you know you can find it)

(ne'er before were the Phoenicians here) (but there
they are) (pulling up in drydock) (where a warehouse)
(has been patiently waiting for them to come in)
(tin is what the Phoenicians have to trade)
(we can vowelize with them for a while)
(tin weeps) (that's one thing it does)
(because of where we were we could always see sparks
from the welders' torches working on the oil rigs)
(we could see them in the distance from our windows)

(which we preferred to have open when we could)
(riata sustained) (amanita sustained) (aught sus-
tained) (standardization endured) (as if we were
modules) (low-grade) (extremely slow motion vertigo
sustained) (imbalance endured) (it's called a pro-
tective slope) (you can call it overprotection) (if
you think it is) (a moat for a moat for a moat)
(lock for a lock) (a combination of something) (you
missed and something you likely didn't want to

miss further) (like a pretty steady ferry)
(in a steamy steady rainfall) (we'll get to the land-
ing by nightfall) (along around midnight we'll be
in our blankets) (we'll have our heads down in all
the right places) (we'll lose our backbones)
(it was as if we were out of proportion) (but to what
that was not in the picture) (you have the camera)
(point it at something) (you have the solution)
(you can try to dissolve it in a slurry of in-

activity) (radio back to us in a few thousand years)
(reach an agreement) (staunch, steep, fearless, sus-
taining) (unbreakable) (fierce, pressing, unbleeding)
(we were sparring partners then) (we walked in wing-
tips) (you've got the tintypes) (you were the one
who dismantled the templates) (there wasn't any
convincing status to calculate) (there were thought-
substitutes available) (approachable) (affordable)
(little side-effects) (minimal collateral damage)

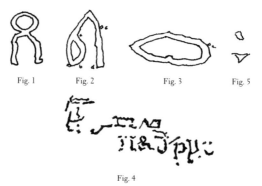

Fig. 1 Fig. 2   Fig. 3   Fig. 5

Fig. 4

(we walked over the borderland) (to where rivercane
hid where the river was)
(it was just a homemade flat-bottom boat but it worked
all right)
(we didn't use oars) (we used poles)
(there was clean water in two canteens)
(we'd spent the night before) (in a ghost town)
(the night before that) (in a cottonwood grove)
(with a flock of caracaras) (with too many snakeskins)

(to look for a house to live in) (to see yourself in
it) (to cross its threshold) (to be or not to be absorbed)
(looking back at what you left behind) (looking back
over into where you once were) (you can be a ghost there)
(you can make it look like a cross section) (and never
see how it started) (and what went on during most of it)
(or hear the end of it) (though someone wrote it down)
(with lots of semiquavers in it) (now and then some
slurs) (and at least once crescendo) (a great grey owl

who looked a little cross-eyed) (and one small time
dot for your trouble)
(ditto for what wasn't yours)
(loco for all those things yet to arrive)
(it's never worked to put a lodestar) (on a layaway
plan anyway)
(lame brain) (lamentable) (laying on of hands)
(it was a vanguard-phase) (like a plunging neckline)
(it was marked with too many arrows)

(it was literally literal)
(like a smoking jacket on a loggia)
(if you stand on a chair in the loggia) (you can see
the fields of tobacco)
(I'd call it a dress depression)
(take it in for an overhaul)
(it had practically been smocked) (to death)
(they don't smock flags)
(or do they sometimes)

(oh it was almost nothing) (like a light depression)
(like light artillery)
(there is a ghost word out there) (somewhere meandering
around)
(betwixt a sawmill) (a smokestack) (a duckblind)
(everything seemed to be infiltrated) (with some kind
of gerrymandering mind) (all crabwise)
(that's why we left the porch light on a tripswitch)
(so as not to play havoc with the insects)

(we did a few things quite thoughtfully)
(at night when we moved from the woods into the
clearing we watched where we walked)
(there were whip-poor-wills there)
(I want to go back up in the hills where those giant
turbine windmills are)
(for a while the kids used the abandoned car) (for a
playhouse)
(I don't think they noticed mice used it with them)

(you gotta) (do) (what you gotta) (do) (usually makes someone
shiver)
(there goes one)
(there goes one in a seersucker sunsuit)
(all decked out)
(there goes one) (where it's raining cats & dogs) (with
a fine black poncho on)
(there goes one in flip-flops tying a knot) (in a
fishing line)

(there go a murmur of them) (all in string-ties)
(it happened during the last loud-speaker phase)
(we missed the parade) (but heard it lasted a long, long)
(time) (unit by unit on into eternity) (like chewing)
(their problem was they took real estate too literally)
(one could feel the avarice for the locus) (amidst the
endless brouhaha) (of some of thc malcontents)
(I was going down to zero again)
(I was going down to sweep out the chicken coop)

(so barn owls could look in some other direction)
(we walked over planks wherever water was)
(in the aftermath of the storm) (we were without
lights) (we turned a generator on)
(that was when an ash went into a tear duct)
(that was our excuse then)
(now it's possible to need to be misted) (like a
fern) (that's been in a room with a heater on)
(not like a hothouse fern) (not like dust for brains)

remnants of Hannah

(sweetbead skirts around everything ceramic)
(ceramics held hold of the temperature of it all)
(it gave it up as the day changed) (since the wind
seemed confused) (it was disorganized) (it was going
to stay) (and then it wasn't) (the hinges were working
overtime) (they were doing double-duty) (all of the
shutters were shut down) (they were trembling)
(we put things away for safe-keeping) (as if we'd
never see them again) (as if they were camouflaged)

(as if they were never sleeping) (it's a bedroom)
(there's a bed in it) (someone's bathrobe thrown
over a chair where they left it) (someone's hair-
brush) (picture frames) (with all of the pictures
removed) (a stack of music standing straight up in a
corner) (it was gone-torn) (it was leave-sore) (it was
fadeaway-laden) (it was minus-shot) we had no for-
ceps for it) (we couldn't say what its make was)
(we didn't know its model) (we couldn't name its

enamel) (we were nameblind) (we were off-guard)
(we were made of terra cotta) (we were ironstone)
(we were castiron) (it was passed down) (you could
see where they'd worn themselves into its edges)
(as if stirring were what they were born for)
(we were staring at what we were stirring) (it
was closing in on us) (it was coming around again)
(we were standing in a courtyard) (you were the
judge) (you were the oath) (you were a fountain)

(twigs were floating around on your surface)
(there were too many wishes in me) (you were
want-starred) (you were wist-ridden) (it felt
like a forced landing) (we were nostomaniacs
for a while) (nothing could stop us) (not even
sandbags) (not even necklaces) (not even night-
caps) (we were unswerving) (we were like trape-
zoids) (eventually we would cross paths) (we
might not be in the same timeframe) (it's a

manger) (it has grain in it) (if you can manage)
(if you still have your wire cutters) (we can
pull it behind us) (we can carry things in it)
(that was when we were force-fed) (we hadn't
hidden our mouths right) (it was as if our teeth
glowed in the dark) (we were frightening) (we
looked emaciated) (we'd been partitioned) (we
had no enclave) (we were stalagmites) (we were
soda straws) (it was dark where we were) (we

couldn't get out of there) (we took our flints
out) (we took off our bracelets) (we were un-
licked) (we hadn't found our alignment) (we were
no-shows) (you had better things to do) (you
couldn't be bothered) (you were my brother) (you
had a sister) (we said we were nailmakers)
(they said they were hammers) (you said pail)
(stone) (rubbish) (you said trash) (rock) (bucket)
(as if you'd come from different sides of an island)

(we were dislocated) (we were distance-glazed)
(we'd been broadcast) (we had no traction)
(we had on iceshoes) (and they were melting)
(we needed some new clamps) (we sounded like
palm leaves) (when our teeth were chattering)
(because we were shivering) (we'd lost our
sweaters) (we'd lost our phonelines) (we had
no locomotion) (if it wasn't nailed down it was
going) (there was no other way to get out of the cur-

rent) (we couldn't be extricated) (no one had
any tongs then) (they weren't status symbols
at that time) (we were like scorpions) (nobody
wanted to touch us) (we were at-large then)
(then we were wherever we wanted to be) (then
we just blended in) (we wanted to be invisible)
(then it was as if we'd never been born) (it was
before our time) (we went back a long way) (then
we were cowpaths) (we were very logical in those

days) (we saw how one thing led to another)
(we knew how spoons worked) (we saw what storms
do) (we knew what glass was) (we pretended we
needed glasses) (it helped us get into character)
(we always avoided the cellar) (you said a fox
lived down there) (you said you didn't say that)
(we knew where you hid things) (when you weren't
looking we'd find them) (you were excavators)
(we had no party system) (no one voted for us)

there was a blue light filtering through a keyhole

(they were bathing) (beside Europe's tallest
waterfall)
(it wasn't a day like any other day)
(it certainly was the front of a horse) (though its
head was hidden)
(we walked on a path through the woods pretty far)
(to the point where the water started)
(you know the physical sensation) (you feel) (as words
curve back around) (to reconfigure something) (you once

supposed you believed)
(the blouse came out of the basin) (a completely
different color)
(I haven't dyed anything that I know of) (in too many
years)
(I'll go find something to dye) (for tomorrow)
(in the middle of last night) (I listened to a son of a
physicist) (tell why a coat of varnish needs to be given)
(to any painted surface worth its paint)

(through a corner of your eyes)
(through a haze of smoke)
(through the longest tunnel on the planet)
(with no place to turn around in it)
(and no end to it)
(one by one they were being pulled) (in so many different
directions)
(were we to keep heading where it looks as if we are)
(going) (eventually we'll wind up) (back where we started)

(when the world was flat) (that didn't happen)
(some of the dripstone in the blue caverns) (glowed
in the morning)
(everything made more sense) (next to the natural
bridge)
(it was tight going with the tom-toms) (into the grottoes)
(without you) (it would have been too much for me)
(with me dripping wet) (with my shirt on inside out)
(without the trade winds)

(we posted a look out near the escarpment)
(with the map unfurled we put push-pins next to the
places) (we would need to remember)
(there could be felt a parabola) (withinward)
(without you everything) (would be lopsided)
(radio waves would all fade away)
(if you wanted to walk) (you had to go barefoot)
(over there where a trough of a wave's) (turning to
spindrift)

(we took the ramp away) (from the crescent city) (to
get to the salt mines)
(how many miles down did we go) (I don't remember)
(I never went anywhere without my sickle)
(you were in charge of the sextant)
(without you) (where would we be)
(we never knew what started) (a sudden oscillation)
(in the tide pools) (maybe an earthquake
maybe) (something about the barometric pressure)

(it certainly seemed to be) (some kind of convoluting
visceral manifestation) (a splinter) (a sting)
(that was the day you rescued me) (from the grotesquerie)
(not that I'd asked to be rescued)
(it left me a little serrated)
(and now whenever I'm feeling somewhat sequestered)
(in a vault all too solo) (like a mothball)
(I put on a necklace) (I put on some boots) (I go to the
window) (I open my eyes to look sideways)

(a solemn vow) (is really severe)
(it is almost like a haircut)
(I wonder whatever happened to the camisole)
(maybe it's in a suitcase) (in the chifforobe)
(and you say what's on your mind) (in the plainest
way) (and it surprises you) (because you didn't know
what you were saying)
(without their crescents fingernails wouldn't look
finished)

(so if it's tactile)
(as if that could be touched) (just barely tapped)
(we found the tambourine) (just clinking to a stop)
(on the wet sidewalk) (underneath a black parasol)
(we found the satchel filled with coins) (without
using dowsing rods)
(we unplaited the drawstrings)
(there was a cold front) (coming to move away the
doldrums) (there were a dozen flashlights) (moving through the
forest)

THERE ARE NINE STAGES

(none of them are where we left them)
(maybe the wind blew them somewhere)
(they were fond of traffic circles) (they built them)
(it was one way of thinking) (but you can't get
very far) (if you stay on a circle forever)
(well) (it feels less certain than crossing a bridge)
(that's a poker face) (it's a soundless soundtruck)
(nobody can find the bottom of that)
(we were standing aside) (we had a viaduct)

(it went around and around hard by an edge of the
rotary) (we could cover it with a pavilion)
(we could distract it with fire birds)
(they were just kids then) (they saluted for the fun
of it)
(they did it with true fidelity) (like pitchforks)
(they tramped right through their firedrills)
(tramped after the bombscares)
(tramped over their sidewalks) (they did it free-hand)

(they didn't even have any guiding stars)
(they didn't even have a full set of funnels)
(they would have to be impromptu) (like glaciers)
(maybe they would find a few handbooks)
(they'd need a squadron of thaumaturges)
(it was slivovitz) (it took out the guesswork)
(that's not translation) (why would it need to be
transmogrified) (it was already ugly enough)
(it was slick) (it was pulp) (they were pawns)

(they said they were illuminati)
(we were never given back our hat pins)
(so they sent it off to the rendering house)
(when it came back) (there wouldn't be much there)
(of what it once was) (you wouldn't be able to
recognize it) (they said they were traveling
salesmen) (they were dissimulators) (they sold
bywords) (like bunco artists) (they were in thrall
to officialdom) (it was hackwork)

(and they were very small cotyledons)
(their axis of revolution was not there)
(they had no axis of symmetry) (it was confusing)
(it was like having a series of too many concussions)
(we were stuck in a go-between situation)
(the rumors came down the mountains)
(it was the world's tallest waterfall)
(in other words it was twicetold)
(it was siltwork, it was sudsy, it was frothful)

(it never felt right to feel like a by-product)
(we took the causeway) (it was longer)
(we could wait for things to transfigure)
(we could look) (for sound advice) (we could sit
under a hemlock in a windstorm and listen)
(we could go stay by some wetlands)
(we've already tried that)
(it was bedlam)
(we left with our eardrums blistered)

(we looked corrugated) (like we were washboards)
(what did they mean by nipped in the bud)
(you're not left with a leg to stand on)
(that's submissive) (that's not salty)
(we could go back to the bayou we came from)
(it's not there anymore) (it's been excised)
(that had some kind of filthy lucre in it)
(whose was it) (it didn't belong to anybody)
(that was all pretend) (like psameads)

(you could see there was part of a stigma)
(it had fallen over) (maybe somebody pushed it)
(were the requiems for it) (there was dark matter)
(we felt as if we were running right beside you)
(we were side by side) (like eyebrows)
(but we couldn't see where we were going)
(we needed our sca legs) (we needed some freesia)
(say you're press agents, show them your flack)
(now filibuster for as long as it takes)

(do some drumbeating) (be immutable) (rend some
garments) (be hardcore) (show some compassion)
(put something out of its misery) (misrender a
little ambivalence) (send it on ice skates)
(it looked trampled) (it wasn't impartial)
(you could see where it was scorched and a trace
of what it was scorched with) (it was ephemera)
(just past the traffic circle comes a penitentiary)
(they say it's empty) (that means it's teeming with life)

ball & chain, mockingbird, the jerk

(that's what it does, it does what you do)
(thus we unfolded our chairs and plainly sat some)
(you move your arm) (its arm moves)
(you sit up straight) (it shifts its position like-
wise) (you lean over to pick up a stick) (it's got
its stick right where yours is when you drop it in
your lap) (you start to say something) (it starts to
say the same thing) (you slow down) (it slows down
with you) (you start to stand) (that's exactly what

it's about to do) (you tell it to stop) (that's what
it tells you) (that's the stubborn fact of it)
(you could vanish) (you could scatter your atoms)
(you could become disembodied for a while)
(what was so fundamental about it)
(it was impersonal on the turnpike it took)
(that's how it stood) (we were related by blood)
(we were luxury items) (we'd been branded)
(we'd been pinpointed, like lab mice) (like lap

dogs) (like terrain maps) (it was a windy radical)
(we were collateral) (widemouthed) (that's the size of
it) (about thirty times wider than three witness
stands) (you stand on your head) (it does what it has
to do to stand on its own) (like a distant relative)
(from another era) (without even a pretext) (apropos
nothing) (it looks like there's a zenith in it
somewhere) (you can see something coiling through
something unwinding through something unflexing)

(we tried to look wilted) (like on nights with no
wind the way flags do) (there was no back and forth)
(nothing reciprocal) (there was no seesaw)
(were we indistinguishable) (I doubt it) (we had
plenty of birdcalls) (we needed that many) (we
needed dead ringers) (everything was oxymoronic
then) (you zazen) (it zazens better than you do)
(like a box or a bag or a bowl of raisins)
(like toothpicks) (they showed us theirs) (they

were ivory) (we found some once) (in a trashpile)
(they said we could keep them) (they said it was turf)
(remember how that sounded) (they said they were
beauty spots) (we were restless) (you twitch and
squirm) (you shift around) (it vellicates with no
problem) (it does it of its own volition) (like a
mindsweeper) (as if it had just been given its
walking papers) (it left nothing to retrace)
(it felt flimsy) (like tracing paper) (you could

make out most of what lay under its surface)
(like clear water) (as if you could drink it
without boiling) (as if it were potable)
(like a love potion) (like pot liquor)
(wear something that will let you blend in with the
merchandise)
(cover yourself with barcodes)
(they were synergists) (they believed in the
Holy Ghost) (they set pigeons on fire)

(you turbinate) (it does the same thing)
(you walk on a shoreline) (pretend you're looking
for driftwood) (be monotonous) (stay under the
radar) (look as if you know where you're going)
(we'd been wiled into this area) (we were witched
into this) (show them your fine-toothed comb)
(say you've been numbed) (let them feel your pins
and needles) (give them your wickiup) (say that's
okay) (you can restock) (and they can restock too)

(one of them was a trigger-happy tree surgeon)
(remember how bad the weeping willows behaved)
(you cried when they hauled them away) (it was
my kingdom) (I kept my horses there) (they were
spotted) (we weren't exactly taking a backroad)
(one of them felt all simpatico with conscription)
(they called it winnowing) (it was torchwood)
(you were supposed to want to be simulacra)
(see if you can make yourself cry real tears)

(it was severe) (like a tango)
(you were plumbed) (you were chorded) (you left
your shoes by the door) (you were well-regarded)
(like starshine) (see if you sound like a turbo-fan)
(you were role-playing) (you were supposed to be a
vagabond) (you were well-traveled) (you were always
losing things) (there was too much to keep up with)
(simulating wasn't one of our options) (we weren't
uniform, we were disorderly) (choppy) (ragged)

And if thou ever happen that same way
To travell goe to see that dreadful place

(we were dipping (our heads) inside of) (one
another's heads) (we came up looking) (as if we'd
been lapping) (water out of a bucket) (or from
a riverbank) (or a basin) (we were true thirsty
animals) (we came up looking) (off into the dis-
tance) (to see if anything was coming) (we needed
to notice) (we were bowing) (into where) (one
another bowed) (giving one another) (concussions)
(when our timing belts were broken) (when we were

losing concentration) (it was escaping) (all of our
escape hatches were open) (as open as a gate) (can
be open) (to get into or out) (of a cemetery) (with
a fence all around it) (fence with an unclear pur-
pose) (fence to unfrighten) (children) (not children)
(they're holding their breaths) (they're looking for
black shutters) (trying to see) (who can concentrate
the longest) (staring at one another) (to see who
will) (blink first) (think fast) (fast longest) (who

will) (find something) (before anyone else can find
it) (get somewhere) (before anyone else) (gets there)
(all for nothing) (because they could do it) (as
natural) (it was to them) (as their breathing) (we'd
seen where) (almost with no exceptions) (all of the
roads we were taking) (were connected) (to one another)
(in one way or another) (from sea) (to shining sea)
(as they were singing) (they were waving) (little flags)
(on sticks) (in front of one another's faces) (they

were) (standing on the steps) (of the capitol)
(engaging) (in) (an act) (of mass hypnosis) (they'd
been deposited) (inside a labyrinth) (there were
strings) (connected) (to all of their buttons) (they
were tangled) (they were star-spangled) (up) (in red)
(white) (and blue) (you said we needed) (to capture
the flag) (there were so many of them to capture)
(there were flags everywhere) (in their windows)
(on their fenceposts) (over their overcoats) (em-

bedded in their hats and shoes) (it was a lucrative
undertaking) (they were draping flags) (over their
coffins) (they were sleeping) (with flags) (next to
their pillows) (under our pillows) (is where we kept
a handful of bullets) (we kept our rifle) (in the
room) (where we were sleeping) (in the corner) (be-
hind a door) (we didn't use it very often) (mostly
we used it for practice) (we'd shoot at tin cans)
(as they floated by) (on a river) (I think we made

up) (I think we dreamed up) (a river of music) (to
cover up something) (so we wouldn't notice) (what
was happening) (it was all or nothing) (we were being
blown backwards) (time was escaping) (it was running
away from us) (once we were) (very good horses) (we
didn't run backwards) (we were very straight-forward
horses) (we didn't know any farriers) (we hadn't
kicked) (a single farrier) (in the chest then) (we
were wild horses) (our manes were on fire) (not the

kind of fire) (that can hurt you) (we were flying
horses) (not the kind on a carousel) (no one wanted
to put a baby on us) (we didn't cruise around) (in
circles) (accompanied by calliopes) (we didn't giddy-
up) (there were no whoas at that time) (there were
no fences) (we didn't have to look out) (for barbed
wire) (electric fences) (hadn't been) (invented)
(we were freewheeling horses) (no one could catch
us) (there was no one around) (who wanted to do so)

(we did our own breeding) (it was thorough enough)
(for us then) (there were no) (vets yet) (we were
always dying) (of natural causes) (there were very
few causes then) (and untimely) (accidents) (our
natural enemies) (were few) (and far between) (you
were a jetblack one) (I was appaloosa) (we were
very peace-loving horses) (we were avoiding some-
thing) (the force of gravity) (wasn't so strong then)
(birds flew more often) (rain wasn't so predictable)

(our hair was more interesting) (pennants weren't)
(working so hard) (to be noticed) (to call attention)
(to themselves) (wind was in) (a fairly relaxed state)
(trees mostly stayed where they started) (these were
pretty steadfast trees) (they hadn't been turned in-
to gallows or weapons) (they weren't toothpicks)
(there were rumors of music) (in their branches)
(from out of their treetrunks) (we hid in a hollow
one one time) (birds were weaving in & out of their canopy)

it looked as if it were time for a little praxis

(there was a navigable channel)
(we'd searched for and found) (a suitable junk)
(very few very seldom seek pleasure) (in shellgames)
(there are so many so varied) (uses for prayer beads)
(some not so good) (some are choking hazards)
(when low tide arrives) (we'll gather on the shoals)
(we'll do that) (in order to install some cargo)
(not much) (a few trunks) (a couple of gunny sacks)
(a catapult) (a highchair) (a birdcage) (a whistle)

(a few missing links) (some straw) (a flint and
a gyroscope) (a jack knife) (a helicopter) (not a
real one) (a prototype) (a very small one) (a
soapdish) (torpedoes) (a doorknocker) (some flippers)
(we will be a shoal) (on a shoal) (we will be a mirror)
(image) (an echo as hindsight is not like an encore)
(did you remember to stow return tickets) (in plain
view) (I did) (I buried them near a blue distyle)
(I took them there in a buckboard)

(I was feeling weakly ductile)
(the hypersonic ideograms) (were causing whiplash)
(all because of a misemployed ideamonger's motor-
mouth) (and so forth)
(I'd like to lie down on some broadloom)
(next to something warm-blooded)
(it could be in the springtime)
(there could be bluebirds in flight tattooed
above all their nipples)

(one of several good places to get to)
("Concealment would make it quite impossible
to estimate whether there is any genuine feeling,")
(speaking of friendship)
(today in plain English)
(it seems like a good translation)
(a good edition)
(a classic)
(inexpensive)

(though not incombustible)
(incivism can get you clobbered)
(it was almost impossible) (to find a hat tree)
(sturdy enough) (to hang our biohazard suits on)
(so mostly we just dropped them where they'd
fall) (in with our t-shirts) (and knapsacks and
old homework)
(we pretty much all looked alike) (in those things)
(that was one thing)

(you know how it goes in the summer) (if you leave
your porch light on) (you look out in the morning)
(and there) (is a shoal of dead June bugs)
(maybe you heard them thwacking themselves out
of their minds through the evening)
(but it didn't register)
(it was in the background)
(what was happening never came to the surface)
(there was no ulterior motive) (no?) (none whatso-

ever) (if there were who'll ever know it)
(they were sheathing things that didn't need
sheaths) (it gives you something to do) (it's
a luxury like leaning on a lamppost) (like leaning
on a friend's shoulder) (like leaning over a guard-
rail) (it gives me vertigo) (then go worship something)
(I'm not going to go there without company)
(then see if you can find a friend to go with you)
(no) (vertigo can be lethal)

(it is self-winding)
(it comes with seven vaults) (all different sizes)
(it is absolutely guaranteed not to misfire)
(it takes care of itself)
(is it self-cleaning)
(it fits in a suitcase)
(it never needs ironing)
(it's heirloom quality)
(it is like a rusty injection)

(the moon's full tonight) (full of reluctancy)
(it lights up the sweet vernal grass) (it looks at
veronica) (it vouches for the water in the channel)
(we can trade the junk for some pirogues)
(I'd like to keep the gyroscope) (if you'll let me)
(keep it) (you seem to need it)
(is sweet vernal grass safe to sleep on?)
(forget about what you did with the tickets)
(love breaks apart in waves)

there were thousands of bats sleeping under the bridge

(it was a snapshot) (it was a relic)
(we were nocturnal from now until sun up)
(eventually your eyes will adjust) (give them time)
(just stand there) (don't move around)
(just be radiotransparent) (and try to remember
something inconsequential)
(I looked in the suitcase) (it was covered with
decals) (sheep jumping fences) (girls in midnight
blue velvet dresses with serpentine sashes)

(there were nine pairs of shoes mixed together)
(it looked like a party) (after it happened)
(the ballroom was empty) (there wasn't anything
in it) (it was chilly)
(I used the key you gave me) (it was brittle)
(that's slush) (that's sludge) (that's marshland)
(that's a pallid bat eating a scorpion)
(that's a long-nose) (that's a free-tail) (that one's
fringed)

(I don't know when it was) (it was after the
faithcure)
(they were sloganeers) (it was falderal) (they were
fair-weather)
(like doorknob-rattling) (they went closet to closet)
(they were saber-rattling)
(it's like sonar)
(sometimes they're rabid)
(we took apart the unicycle) (it was useless)

(that's just their home range) (it's not their
territory) (they don't defend it)
(see if you can feel around in the talus)
(you hid the bookmobile in the alley behind the
towering pallets) (why'd you do that)
(it was a reflex)
(like a nimbus) (there was nothing you could do
about it) (is that it)
(I know one place) (to look for the picayune cache)

(that's a passado) (I learned it in nightschool)
(we can sacrifice a little bit of the low visibility)
(if we wear nightgowns)
(you don't want to be phlegmatized) (it's too sob-
ering)
(that's how it felt on the stretcher)
(I remember the inkstain on the front of the hatband)
(some of their wings are translucent)
(is that what you want me to say) (I remember)

(they used shorthand)
(it looked like a flying hand) (but it was a nightlight)
(they made it look like it was old hat) (like it was
outcast) (bailed out of the rowboat)
(it's a dusky membrane) (it's a beauty)
(we can be refluent if we need to)
(it was red-lined) (it was a farrago)
(you look almost handsome in nightshade)
(we need to familiarize the chaparral with ourselves)

(they called it subsistence thinking)
(it was mind-numbing) (I remember it)
(that meant drinking water) (that meant no entry)
(we said we were farmers and farmers we were)
(we worked in snowshoes)
(we were electronic)
(I remember where the horses were standing while
they looked at us through an electric fence)
(here) (take this button) (it's an amulet)

(it shows pretty much how the road winds)
(that's a switchback) (that's a cowpath) (that's a
roach clip) (it's called a hairpin)
(in many instances it has to be stabilized)
(I remember how your hair blew over your eyebrows)
(it blew into your mouth) (you looked puzzled)
(I took the jeep down the runway) (it clattered through
the palmettos) (I couldn't hear myself thinking)
(you stood on the platform) (I couldn't see you)

(it was all crepuscular) (like in a barrel)
(that is a seaplane) (that is a pilgrim) (it might
have been ransacked) (those are the arrows of lust)
(and love as they say in the movies) (as the lights
dim) (as their hands come back to life)
(we were transfixed) (on account of how they flew so
fast) (that was the hindsight) (about like a nightshirt)
(I think we were fasting) (I no longer remember
what we were fasting for)

A door slammed, and the child whirled
his arms through the town square

(it felt like feeling around in the dark)
(in the apex middle) (of any anywise day)
(I'd left you wondering if you'd done the right thing)
(sometimes that's how we always leave one another)
(ajar) (somehow cleaving) (half-way open)
(the superimposition of a new set) (new was what
they called it) (of nomenclature)
(the superimposition of a vast set) (vast was a factor
somewhat upended) (of reckonings)

(we could hear something clicking)
(can you hear where it's coming from)
(sounds as if it might be coming from on high)
(as if someone might be calling)
(as if someone might be whittling with our thinking)
(out there on the edge of town) (in the old store)
(by the woodstove where the crackerbarrels roam)
(don't leave your comb there) (nothing with your private
squama on it) (if they find it) (they'll use it)

(it felt like feeling around in a sandbox)
(after a rainsquall) (looking for a babytooth)
(maybe a sandbox is nothing but a pretext)
(I doubt it) (but I don't doubt it always)
(maybe you should look into it)
(after a rainstorm mesquite changes everything)
(it cracks open the ozone) (as if it's been struck
by lightning) (old timers called them screwbeans)
(they weren't trying to hide anything)

(sooner or later we could hear something whirring)
(if you don't pass the test you go in for 10,000
scratch tests)
(we can fan out) (we can double around) (we can meet
back later on the northwest side of the watertower)
(just outside the fence at the northwest corner of
the cemetery) (we spotted when we first flew over)
(it stings) (then it blisters) (it feels as if it
lasts a lifetime)

(last time we looked) (they really were shooting at
fish in a barrel) (weren't they)
(I remember all of their watchchains)
(it felt like scrounging around for icecubes in a
hailstorm)
(everything looked pitted) (like it had been sand-
blasted)
(it sounds as if something's rummaging around
in a wastepaper basket)

(that is a spyglass) (that is a whizbang) (that
is a soothsayer) (that is a white squall) (that is
a waterpipe) (that is scratchpaper) (that is whipcord)
(that is some white space) (that is a crepe myrtle)
(that's a beat-up spikelet) (that's another one)
(that's some wallpaper) (you'll have to look under
it) (that's chamiso) (that's high octane) (that's
war of nerves) (that's cloak & dagger) (that's crack

of doom) (they say it's a watchword) (they want
you to hear it around every corner) (that's a
plain brown wrapper) (that's a hook you can hang
your shirt on) (those are brackets under the shelf
you can have to put what you want on) (those are
two pillows) (that is a lightbulb) (that is a divided
highway) (that is a magazine) (that word is warlike)
(that's watch & ward) (that is a hasp) (that is a
pommel) (that's a doorknob) (that's a key) (that's

a plate) (that's your window) (when it's cold you
can take notes on it) (if you step on the bed you can
crawl out of it) (it's about nine feet down to the
ground) (that's just the furnace) (that man comes
by every day with his dog) (that's one of the half-
tones) (it's always up near the ceiling) (if the phone
rings look in the icebox) (if you need anything you
can call me) (use the tincan) (it's in back of the
birdcage) (we'll have to forage)

(it felt like being screened) (in your sleep
as if the way you'd countersunk was off)
(you could see the callbox) (but you couldn't touch
it) (you wouldn't want to talk into it) (you didn't
know who was on the other end of the line)
(that was the coup) (that was the brink)
(we could hear something gurgling)
(thicker than blood)
(worse than if we knew what to call it)

(And those who saw them off have left the platform)

(we were fairly certain it was a photo-finish)
(it just about happened without anyone knowing)
(over there in that cup of soup (don't let
anyone see you) look) (it's a listening device)
(we talked about the fate of the couch in code)
(most of us liked the sensation of flickering)
(that came as the last few frames of the film
(we were at the movies) (it was a matinee) (it
was a double feature) flew off the reel)

(we'd hidden the boat in some cattails)
(we could come back for it later) (maybe tomorrow)
(my arms were about to fall off) (they'd semaphored
more than they should have)
(so much of the discussion near the quince trees
never paid off) (they were polarized) (though they
never said so)
(one of the movies was set on the Amazon)
(I noticed what happened when we brushed shoulders)

(sometimes you look like a very healthy clematis)
(sometimes like a pencil someone daydreaming has
chewed on) (like one of the green ones made to look
like a snakeskin)
(you can figure out the secret grip by walking
through the city in a snowstorm)
(your alias can be espadrilles)
(mine can be moccasin)
(no wait) (an alarm just went off in my elbow)

(if they say they were talking about Nepali
medicine they weren't)
(I know where there's a culvert that's usually
dry) (you can see the edges of it from the top of
the lighthouse) (see if you can become very good
at reproducing the sound of a foghorn) (it might
come in handy when we go spend some time in the
desert)
(don't sign your name) (use a pawmark)

(for a split second I thought I could see a tachist-
oscope) (I thought you said they didn't use them
anymore) (I thought you said they'd been outlawed)
(I thought you knew about foxglove) (I thought you
said you were not to be quoted)
(it was nothing) (it was just an ink cartridge)
(just say *quo animo* whenever you feel like it)
(and if you need to blend in look like a marmot)
(all of the trumpet vines are programmed to thread

through the secret passages) (so let them)
(if they say they've gone into executive session
make like you don't understand them)
(you don't have to tell them anything past) (your
kingdom phylum class order family genus species)
(you can say you're a glassblower) (you work in a
lab) (say you don't know where it is)
(we can get to the river if we follow the treeline)
(the deer in these parts keep a very neat browseline)

(everything's sensitive)
(you could tell which parts had been dubbed)
(what do you think they were talking about when
they kept talking about alien fish)
(somethings will sometimes be neon) (you be neoteric
whenever you want to)
(there's a vest made of porcupine quills in the attic)
(here's a little sack of grommets)
(you can say you're a groundskeeper)

(I feel more like groundcover) (more like vinca)
(they call it their little hideaway) (though they
don't meant that the same way we do)
(did you say there was some kind of group insurance)
(we were all some kind of runic inscriptions)
(what did you think of the sightgags in the first
part of the movie)
(I hope you remember where you stashed the seismograph)
(it's the only way left) (to figure out asphalt)

(more important than their talking points) (is their
tone of voice) (you said) (talking to yourself) (it wasn't
the slightest movement of an eyelash) (it wasn't a
quiver over an eyebrow) (it was being italicized right
there in front of our eyes) (it looked anemically
pilfered) (like it had been to a bloodbank too many
times) (a bloodbank privately owned by a murderous
doctor) (how long does it usually take to get your sea
legs) (now remind me) (what do we mean when we say *row*)

What are the principal objects of their Worship?

(just where you told me) (where no one could find
it)
(over there) (around that bend) (across that channel)
(that's where driftwood collects) (we can use some)
(if we need it we can drag it up on a sandbar)
(maybe it's cottonwood)
(first thing in the morning we'll go through the
motions)
(those are wolffish)

(you can scrub out the kettle with a handful of
sand)
(that's how they worshipped) (they'd found a god
to dissolve in their mouths) (I never
saw one)
(there's an oildrum next to the driftwood) (we can
find more of them and start a steelband)
(it was a long time ago) (there was still a sound
barrier)

(you told me not to tell anyone)
(there was a hard-wired problem child who'd lost
control of one of the learning curves) (I thought
you told me it was reserved) (for harrowing
rats in a maze) (they've clocked a googol miles
down that particular road) (you look like a cat
thinking about swallowing a canary)
(it's a good covered wagon)
(it's got a lot of roadability)

(say you're a receptionist) (say it's not flesh
and blood) (say it's a memo) (you have no clue
who sent it) (ask them if you can point them in
the right direction) (upstream or downstream)
(to the thirtieth floor) (to the rear of the audi-
torium) (three blocks over) (on the red-eye)
(west of the churchsteeple) (room 639) (you're in
the wrong building) (it's the next one over)
(we can sell you a compass) (or just let you have it)

(if you happen to be experiencing high levels of
sales resistance) (are you allowed to drink coffee)
(not until sundown) (we can make an exception)
(sometimes it acts like a sedative)
(you said keep it a secret until the time comes)
(it was shocking pink) (it was similar to napalm)
(it can turn your skin as weird as this fishskin)
(in the strictest sense it wasn't recoilless)
(they were noisemakers) (they were recidivists)

(at that they were virtuoso)
(loose lips sink ships was what you told me)
(my lips are sealed is what I said back)
(it caught us off-guard) (we had been up on the
high ledges) (it looked like the place was empty)
(we'd been distracted by eagles) (I've never seen
one) (what do they look like)
(we counted almost a dozen)
(we could see dead flowers someone must have hurled)

(up in the hemlocks) (maybe it was loosestrife)
(it might have been wolfbane)
(we could see miles of pylons down in the valley)
(is that pompano or is it redfish)
(they looked kinky and in need of a recall)
(maybe they were mums)
(it was a long time ago) (it came to nothing)
(we ditched the hibachi because it was too heavy)
(they dealt in powerlines) (they made a killing)

(remember the morning you nearly cut off your thumb
chopping kindling)
(you said no matter what you said)
(you said you wouldn't change your mind)
(you said you wouldn't flip-flop)
(it might have made it harder to hitchhike)
(say you're a farrier) (say you shoe horses)
(show them your furnace) (boil them some water)
(you were vacillating) (you could die trying)

(we have a canister of very dry matches)
(they were savvy in some ways)
(except for the ones who drove surreys) (they
weren't paying attention) (remember the surrey
you gave me) (we had to piece it together)
(they liked picnics) (they liked open fires)
(sometimes that's a virtue) (like a cowlick)
(it came with an oath) (you asked me to keep it)
(acacia lashing) (in high winds touched a nerve)

reverse rapture

(we were subterranean then) (it lasted a long time)
(you wore a jacklight) (like a third eye)
(we were spelunkers) (we worked in the crypts)
(and the icemines and the saltmines and the
sewers) (remember the raft we took down there)
(and up in the mountains where the silvermines were)
(remember the time we rounded a corner right in the
middle of a gunbattle) (only one side had guns)
(the other side were birds) (they were pigeons)

(what were pigeons doing roosting underground)
(being shot down from rafters)
(they said it was target-practice) (they said they
were killing a little time) (they were good at it)
(who were they) (they were armed-guards)
(what were they guarding)
(they were in uniform) (they wouldn't tell us)
(they did it for kicks) (it was a perk) (they were
just parked there) (like a kickback)

(sometimes when you walked behind me you made me
doubt my own shadow) (that was not on purpose)
(it was tangential) (not like a bonus)
(we said we were sightseeing) (we said we had
jetlag) (we showed them our strip maps) (we gave
them our passports) (we said we were on our way
to some kind of shivaree) (we needed a sidewalk)
(we said we were shirring) (we said we would shunt
it) (one of us said we were sorry) (we were jerry-

built) (we were tempest-tossed) (we were crusta-
cean) (we needed a shrimp boat) (we'd take a sub-
lease) (we would be temporary) (we still had our
cubicles) (they'd lifted the quarantine) (not in
the dockyards) (we needed a shade tree)
(that was their shoptalk) (we didn't know it)
(maybe we said jamboree) (like a side bet)
(there was so much cryptic gossip down there) (we
needed a speed boat) (to keep up with it)

(we needed some oxygen tanks) (we needed gas masks)
(there wasn't much of a cover-charge)
(it was an earthquake)
(it was melodramatic)
(we felt like a lost cause)
(it was like being a bee stuck in an icecave)
(subsequently) (that's what we'll be)
(it was May 14, 1804) (we mounted our gondolas)
(we unfurled our telescope)

(something I really needed) (got left behind in a
cubbyhole) (but you took it in stride) (like a
parakeet) (like a dice cup)
(not even telekinesis could fix it)
(we'd stored what we'd need) (it was waterproofed)
(it was bone brown) (it was café au lait)
(no) (more like honey) (the dark kind)
(they were paper wasps)
(they were extremely social)

(they made paper) (they didn't make honey)
(say you're a printer) (say you like dingbats)
(start with a bible) (or something like that)
(say you're bogged down in a dialectical mind-
shaft) (say mine-field) (roll up your windshield)
(make it a paradox)
(say it's a telethon) (point to the overpass)
(say it's a subsidiary) (not your main line of
work) (that's how you cover your back)

(with a paper fan) (no less)
(technically it isn't raining) (rain doesn't
happen in these parts)
(it isn't wind) (it's a vacuum)
(like the sunny side) (like a vortex)
(do you think it might be surmountable)
(it is possibly all blue retractable)
(maybe with some kind of hydrofoil)
(that isn't fog) (I don't know what it is)

(it looks like some kind of cover-up)
(as soon as you get to the tunnel start whistling)
(not literally under the volcano) (under its influ-
ence)
(someone said they were mutant royalists)
(that's not the call of the wild) (that's a calliope)
(you can hear it) (it's way off in the distance)
(the eels were pretty friendly when they twined around
our fingers) (that) (that brings to mind a calf's tongue)

a rest from forced marches

(some of them stay underground for seventeen years)
(they emerge singing) (if you can call that singing)
(they leave their husks) (clinging to treetrunks)
(we call them ghostbirds)
(we call them glassphantoms)
(if you can stand to you can crush some and drink
them) (but only with rainwater) (you've collected in
a babyshoe) (and the baby had better be living)
(and you should be standing by a spider lily)

(it's a natural progression from roustabout to
roughneck) (it was like being forwarded)
(you felt as if you were being passed from one hand
to another) (but it wasn't a race) (you weren't a
stick) (it was a way to keep body and soul together)
(if you say so) (it was like sweeping sand on a
sanddune) (you didn't do it for money) (it was spo-
radic) (like a forte) (it didn't seem to do much)
(it could barely keep the wolves from the door)

(they were tight-knit) (it was only natural they'd
be in-grown) (once they were shunned they were shun-
ned for good) (remember what happened when the lode-
star was forsworn) (we were spellbound) (like a round-
house) (it sounded like some kind of chemical) (like
an insecticide) (was it uxoricide) (it almost was)
(they had no sense of valence then)
(they were not splicers)
(they almost never remembered to shut their scissors)

(we were close to a lumberyard) (you could smell
it)
(we made pretty good use of their pallets and fork-
lifts)
(it was how we lived) (we were wayfaring)
(sometimes we were free-floating wicks)
(we could see what we needed) (it was always far off
in the distance)
(out of reach)

(like virga)
(like something you want in a fable)
(you can drag a table up to where you think it is)
(you can stand on it)
(you can have a friend nearby spot you)
(somehow or other)
(you can pretend you don't want it)
(you can make like you're looking for cobwebs)
(as if you're putting a key on a ledge of a doorframe)

(everyone felt feeble for a few days) (or in apogee)
(we needed a switchback) (like a cowpath)
(it was riversand) (it was slippery)
(the keynote address lacked a keystone)
(like an avalanche) (remember the mudslide that al-
most killed us) (we were lucky that day) (we'd been
fishing) (we were fishers though we didn't know it)
(and we were not nearly as superstitious)
(that's why my shirt's) (on inside out) (it has to stay

that way until we get to the floodplain)
(do you think we'll find the highway)
(you can say you're a wrangler) (try to look
windblown) (show them your roughhewn manners)
(show them your bowlegs) (say what you can do
with numbers) (keep them busy)
(give them your business card) (if you have one)
(point them to a brick sidewalk)
(show them your brick)

(do you remember why they pounded bricks into dust)
(was it for some kind of solstice)
(I don't think I ever knew what they were doing)
(we should try to make it to an esplanade) (maybe
we'll find who's sending distress calls)
(it was a wet blanket) (it had gone overboard)
(sometimes they were almost good providers)
(we can use my necklace) (the one of buffalo nickels)
(how come we've never seen you wear it)

(it weighs a ton) (like an iceberg)
(the unwritten laws turned out to be the worst kind)
(they were all about vengeance)
(say you were shipwrecked) (show them one of every-
thing) (show them your lean-to) (let them see you
all tattered) (some of the icebergs are melting)
(what's going on with the subscriptions)
(the sun still had the wherewithal) (it was coaxing)
(four-o-clocks to open) (they were relaxing)

I know that timid breathing.

(the ground was sliding away from under us)
(there were ten-foot poles touching us everywhere)
(as if we'd been caught in a hailstorm)
(with our guard down) (on a proving ground)
(it was rocky) (we were shaky) (we felt like
icecubes) (there was no lair there) (we had no
den then) (there were too many collars)
(we slipped them) (we left them where no one
could find them) (especially we couldn't find

them) (I thought you said we didn't want them)
(we were welders then) (we made sparks fly)
(our masks turned us into some kind of insects)
(we were ants then) (we were straightforward)
(we were dirt-movers) (we were good bone-cleaners)
(we were praying mantises) (we were efficient)
(we were cannibals) (it was uncanny) (we were
at the mercy of tactical angels) (they were
vigilantes) (they were zealots) (they threw

zeroes around like crazy) (like they were collars)
(it's a cabinet) (so open it) (open it slowly)
(it's filled with bottles) (they're filled with
liquids) (liquids are for strangers) (they wanted
to claim their ancestors) (they wanted to walk
one behind the other) (they wanted to stand side-
by-side) (to be in a bucket-brigade) (but there
was no flood) (there was no fire) (they were building
pyramids) (they were mining for something) (they'd

had their brains sealed) (that was a near miss)
(this amounts to a kind of immunization) (it's a
homeopath's dream scheme) (it smells like rocket
fuel) (keep your flints down) (don't say any-
thing incendiary) (there where there's cant there)
(there was little cantabile about it) (they
weren't singing) (they were storing up ammunition)
(it was a kind of status-seeking) (they were
lever beavers) (their dens were very complicated)

63

(and their plans were all for sale) (we need
some cantilevers) (we need to alleviate something)
(we are going down in an elevator) (this is a
close shave) (it wasn't as if we appeared out of
nowhere) (it was a mindset) (they were all roosters)
(they'll end up in stewpots) (just one will be left)
(just one booster rooster) (bringing the sun up)
(lighting the sky) (so we can see one another)
(so our skin can change colors) (so we can walk

under umbrellas) (so we can reactivate the parasols)
(we need some shade trees) (we need chinaberries) (we
need a mimosa) (with its pink sticky flowers)
(and good limbs to roost on) (and its fizz frenzy)
(and its riot gear) (and its ultra-canonical security)
(it was a club then) (it was all claviform)
(they were clucking) (like they were brooding)
(we were in very close quarters) (like they were
clubable) (we needed a keyboard) (we needed some

soul-stirring music) (they were all out of
anthems) (they were fighting over the inheritance)
(they wanted the baubles) (they wanted the homestead)
(it was like being tangled in under a Portuguese
man-of-war) (with stingrays for company) (and you
hadn't had any choice in the matter) (they bap-
tized the dead) (they clubbed baby seals) (they
were motherfuckers) (and what's the corollary
to that) (we were better off being orphans)

(not knowing where we came from) (to whom we owed
allegiance) (where we got our sharp clavicles from)
(it was a posse) (the dispatch was summary) (we
were down-and-out) (we were on the streets) (we
were blistered) (we were stonewalled) (they
kept sheep in us) (and snakes liked to lie in the
sun on us) (and ants and spiders and centipedes
went in and out of us) (we were permeable)
(we had gooseflesh) (we were acting like stoics)

(you never learned to ride a bicycle) (you were
stubborn) (you were born that way) (it made you
beautiful) (like ants in amber) (that was a
necklace too hard to wear) (it weighed more than
a cinderblock collar) (you couldn't fly with it)
(you couldn't float on your back all day on a pond
with it on) (you couldn't run as fast as you
wanted to when you were with it) (it took justice
into its own hands) (suspiciously) (like an octopus)

For the PRECESSION of the Equinoxes is improving.

(it's scaffolding) (it's supposed to be temporary)
(the domino effect) (had been forgotten about)
(it was in storage) (nobody knew where)
(that's a logging road) (you can see its gutters)
(they leave handprints) (they shudder with dolor)
(nobody could settle on any particular color)
(they meant different things to different people)
(for luck) (on the cheap) (stop now) (flesh for sale)
(fresh fruit) (insect free) (aquafarm) (moon control)

(it was label-resistant) (nobody knew how to embroider
it) (it felt like hailstones) (big as tombstones)
(it strained everyone's intelligence) (we had tooth
problems) (we'd been flying too much) (our edges
were curling) (we were like silt over sand) (we felt
as if we were sugar dissolving in lime juice) (it
was heavy-handed) (we were covered with treadmarks)
(it was cosmetic) (like crystal handcuffs) (we were
fish then) (we wanted our ladders) (most of them were

rotten) (we can cut down some trees and build new
ones) (we can contrive it out of convection)
(say you're a weatherman) (seed them some clouds)
(remember how it felt to be scuds on a mountain)
(we had good motivations) (like treeroots buckling
up sidewalks) (we worked like treeroots) (we'd go
anywhere looking for water) (we were hydrologists
then) (we had stewpots) (we were fast-breaking)
(we were aerosol) (we had currency) (we were paper

airplanes) (our creases were in all the right places)
(we hadn't been stratified so many times) (it was
because they were eye-minded) (they couldn't see us)
(we weren't eyefuls) (we were just something to take
note of when they weren't working) (we were like
scrimshaw) (you were one of the ones covered with flags
and lady liberty) (she was an eyeful) (we were hay
rolls) (then we were haywire) (we needed paperweights)
(we needed dollys) (it was money-laundering they did

as a sideline) (one little cooking fire stirred up
all of that cloudcover) (we were walking through a
ghosttown) (it was a terrestrial globe) (it wasn't
any bigger than an eyeball) (it was at the bottom
of a fishbowl) (there weren't any fish in it) (the
water was gone) (and it looked as if it had been con-
signed to oblivion) (do you still have it) (it's
somewhere around) (we tried to put it in a safe place)
(in one of the treetrunks) (act like a lumberjack)

(show them your blue ox) (your animal companion)
(show them the marks left where you merged)
(they said they were covered with scruples)
(they needed some tearlifts) (you can seed them
with dryice) (that will use up all of the liquid
assets we have left) (then we can sell off some of
the dunking contraptions) (we don't need them)
(we can act the way hummingbirds act) (we can fight
the way hummingbirds fight) (you can wear your red

vest) (you can wear your red cowboy hat) (it looks
awful) (as if it were made for television) (the
worst kind) (remember the scripts that were written
to teach us something) (past the stratosphere the
sky isn't blue anymore) (we were unteachable)
(we were woodblocks) (we lived in a sawmill)
(when there was lightning) (it nearly burned down)
(we were unwashed) (we were scoured) (we felt untouch-
able) (and somewhat equivocal again in our science)

(you were always exact to me) (like a storm cellar)
(I liked it near your airstreams) (you never called
me a social parasite and I felt good about that)
(you never said things like the handwriting is on the
wall) (you never said we were biding our time) (you
weren't a warden) (you weren't a damper) (you didn't
live in a chimney) (you didn't work for management)
(we were still under construction) (there were
warning signs all over us) (in that shocking pink

orange) (like we'd been pickled) (as if we were beets
or some other kind of root vegetables) (you weren't
a gladiator) (you weren't resistant) (you weren't
a virus) (you didn't know what a firewall was)
(sometimes you did do a little fire-breathing)
(not like a firebrand) (more like a fire that some-
one banked in the evening waiting around until
morning) (there were streets of clouds over the
plains) (we were ice crystals) (laboratory grade)

— fertile (?) mud.

(what is it) (it is coming up from somewhere)
(with tangled hair) (with eyes) (without having seen
the light of day for what looks like a long time)
(it looks like a live one) (from somewhere we couldn't
see) (we'd never been there) (like that rusty old
boot you've been dragging behind you) (it's erasing
my footprints) (and leaving mine right where I left
them) (with their soles sewn on backwards) (it made
you look just a shade taller) (they were trailers)

(they were waiting for someone to put something on
them) (they were like slides) (there were mules
standing in front of them) (it was another long
day) (the icecubes had all melted) (we'd been
eating thistles) (we dipped them in vinegar)
(we carried a jar of it around in our pockets)
(as if they were thinking) (their thoughts were
changing colors) (as soon as they'd reach air-
contact) (as soon as they'd drifted sufficiently)

(say you're a taxidermist) (say you're all out of
eyeballs) (say you're not too particular) (show
them your icechest) (show them the legs of your
tweezers) (we used them to remove splinters)
(we were traumatized) (we'd lost our bearings)
(like we were three sheets to the wind) (we'd lost
our clothespins) (we couldn't find our spitcups)
(we had no trammels) (we didn't want them) (we
didn't want their twitches) (we needed some spine-

guards) (we needed life-preservers) (they called
everything indicators) (it was a kind of lassitude)
(they were all out of friendship) (it was too hard
to have some) (there was no other) (they couldn't
ramify) (they had to talk to themselves) (they
had to hear themselves think) (they were memorized)
(they had more memory than they knew what to do with)
(that's quicksand) (that's the tarpits) (that's
a strap) (that's a single-blade razor) (that's

lather) (those are andirons) (those are embers)
(that's paper burning) (those are leaves on fire)
(it's the top of a manhole) (it weighs too much
to carry) (leave it) (right where we found it) (some-
one could fall into there) (and that would be the
end of it) (they could find their way out) (it might
take them a long time) (they could stay together)
(they could tie ropes to themselves) (to keep them-
selves in unison) (to figure it out together) (to

reach some kind of understanding) (to stay under
the radar) (to be above it all) (right in the thick
of it) (next to an oaktree) (next to a pantry)
(under a ceiling) (up in a corner) (it was hanging
upside down) (you could see it breathing) (it was
alive then) (it might still be alive now) (now is
a backstop) (now is a coaltrain) (now is a window-
frame) (where has its glass gone) (it's right where
we left it) (it's jagged) (it has its own splinters)

(it was demagnetized) (so it just sat there)
(like it had been frozen) (it was freeze-dried)
(you were my friend then) (you were my lover)
(you were a safehouse) (you were an asylum)
(you were an archive) (you were not in any par-
ticular order) (you were always exchanging places)
(we were wheels then) (we were on casters)
(we were kinetic) (we were hard to keep track of)
(you left some traces) (we had scattered our data)

(we searched) (the high heavens) (your biorhythms
were barely detectable) (you were subtle)
(you were agile) (we were almost goats then)
(we ate your shirttails) (we climbed around in a
storehouse) (we knocked some things down) (off the
shelves) (we were practicing) (we were in agree-
ment) (we were a squad then) (we went through the
squalls with our shoes on) (we tunneled through
snowbanks under moonlight) (you built a city there)

(it was your town) (you said what went on there)
(you put who you wanted to see there) (they were
free agents) (they weren't robots) (you could see
their minds working) (it was on their faces)
(the way gravity works on a windowpane) (there was
a certain amount of distortion) (and emotional
extortion sometimes creeped in) (when we weren't
paying attention) (say you're a streetsweeper)
(show them your brushes) (your slow steady progress)

radiant heat

(they were talking about skin grafts) (we were
thinking about orange trees) (we were making an
attempt to look around in music) (as if it were
a space to fill) (but it was always moving) (and
it was inside somewhere) (and we were inside some-
where ourselves) (that's what they said) (they said
they didn't like stories within stories) (they
didn't like nesting boxes) (russian dolls made
them seasick) (they were backing themselves into

a corner) (and there was wet paint creeping) (slowly)
(like a glacier) (almost surrounding everything)
(their heads were huge) (but it was mostly bone)
(it looked as if there were a lot of room in it)
(as if it were waiting to be re-filled) (as if they were bottles)
(or propane tanks or oillamps) (mantles on mantels)
(inside facing mirrors) (they were going
on forever) (to a limit) (to a degree) (that is a magnetic
needle) (it floats on water) (it points to somewhere) (that's

a laser) (it has very beautiful eyelashes) (it
cuts clear across a causeway) (to where we find
arrowheads) (where there's no swimming for still
a few more hours) (where wet sand is) (where hands
hurt touching fireworks) (you were always standing
off somewhere where shade was) (you were paying
attention to something) (you were watching) (there
were wristbands everywhere on you) (you were made
of snakeskin) (you were grommeted) (you were an

73

eyelet) (you had bronze eyes) (you didn't want
to be bonsaied) (you just wanted to be normal)
(that was a mantra) (it was like floating all
evening on a relatively peaceful body of water)
(then came the ground swell) (we didn't see it
coming) (it turned us over) (we asked to be
turned over) (we were just done on one side)
(we were crisp there) (we helped shoemakers)
(the leather kind) (the ones with lasts on their

tables) (the ones who put the shoes in shoes)
(our crust wasn't stable) (our crumbs were falling
out) (grosbeaks were following us) (birds were
taking us away) (we were larva manna) (we were
snow models) (there was lazurite in us) (it was
majestic) (dazzling) (magnificent) (we were ground
work) (we were raw material) (we were still rare
then) (we could be turned into other things) (we
had tunnels in us) (where you could hide things)

(we were crypts then) (there were too many bones
in us) (we had more skulls than we knew what to do
with) (we needed equipoise) (there was none of
that stuff anywhere near here) (it hadn't been
invented yet) (nobody had found any) (so we wept
instead when we spent time with one another)
(that's all we knew how to do) (it was our music)
(then we exchanged all of our earthly possessions)
(we were relaying cryptogram ponies) (we were cry-

babies) (floating on lava) (floating on rafts
down a river) (there was nothing stopping us)
(we had no cork trees) (our bark hadn't been
taken away from us) (no one had carved their
initials in us) (no one loved one another into
us) (we had no hearts then) (we were empty)
(we had well-functioning tearducts) (cross talk
never slowed us down) (we were focused on our
purpose) (we were telescopes) (we had many

lenses) (that's how we found one another) (we
would lose one and then we would lose another)
(we were like shoes then) (you'd see us by the
sides of highways) (there were crows on us)
(they were leather-lunged) (they woke us up in
the morning) (they were our alarm clocks) (we
were sleep-deprived) (so we would be able to
answer their questions) (but we didn't speak
the same language) (and the translators were

pretty tricky) (we never understood their motives)
(we said that in sign language) (with just the
barest flicker of an eyelid) (we were mind readers)
(we read one another's minds) (we were talking to
one another the same way shadows carry on their
conversations) (better versions of us) (us less
lumpy) (us less so needy) (us not so useless)
(us with no clothes on) (before we were skin)
(we were hiding under fire escapes) (smoking)

The sands are frantic
in the hourglass.

(some were more frazzled than others) (more
a frayed way they had on their edges) (they were
roughcut) (they were ragged) (it made them look
expensive) (it was a practice) (as if they were
living in lawsuits) (as if they were passing
through sickrooms) (rooms with crooked straws
on their tables) (full of oaths) (loaded with
swearing) (with syringes and little wooden hammers)
(as if something were under construction)

(you gave me your word of honor) (your honor)
(for the purpose of) (in order to) (for the sake
of) (some flimflam) (to set up a franchise)
(there was quality control built right into it)
(they wanted french fries) (we were as fried
as they were)
(we were sizzling) (we were bathing in chemical
baths) (it was supposed to make us much better)
(at the end of the day we would have a much

better frame of reference) (we would be inside
one) (one with a cot and a bucket and one bare
light bulb) (cold rations) (we would not be
allowed to talk with one another then) (only
on their terms) (they wanted us to be termites)
(to take down buildings) (to follow woodgrain)
(to be eyeless) (to be caste-bound) (to know
what's expected) (you're expected to do) (and do
it ceaselessly without thinking) (we needed

some smugglers to get us out of this business)
(some coyotes) (we needed armadillos) (you were
already) (long through our escape hatch) (you
took our escape mechanisms with you) (you left
a referee) (and turned into an angleworm) (you
said to meet you at the trout farm) (our weather
is under a trance) (of remnants of other storms)
(you were an enlisted man) (there was nothing
left of your uniform) (not even remnants of a

haircut) (not one cell of your skin) (no noise
of your voice) (you were fleckless now) (you
were with the noiseless file) (now) (you were
out there) (you were done practicing) (we stood
around looking at one another in headphones)
(but they weren't attached to anything) (we looked
as if we had headcolds) (we were all hangdog)
(we were all tongue-tied) (we were tearworn)
(we were sorry-tired) (we were bone sore)

(we wanted our beds back) (we wanted to be seeds
again) (to stick our necks out) (to turn into
taproots) (to fall through the cracks) (to crack
open something) (we were husk piercing) (our
armature wasn't with us any more) (we were standing
next to an armored car) (we weren't guarding it)
(we weren't trying to break into it) (we were just
there by accident) (we weren't thieves then)
(it was past curfew) (that's when you hit the am-

bulance) (there was somebody in it) (we never
saw them) (we didn't even know it was happening)
(we were en route somewhere else) (that's what
you told us) (we always knew you were up to some-
thing) (as you were) (we were timekeepers then)
(we were stovepipes) (we were sewing umbrellas)
(it felt as if it were drizzling where we were)
(as if infinitesimal needles were landing on us)
(you were in lifeboats) (by this time)

(we were jittery) (a hustler was jostling us)
(we needed to go away from where the get-goers
were) (from where the go-getters rambled) (to
avoid being trampled) (that was perpetual)
(like presto) (like jingo) (like there were more
pressing matters) (it was like being crowded
into a room) (there wasn't an inch to move)
(with too many crescendos) (it was a gruesome
congruence) (there shellgames mixed into it)

(we were halfway conscience stricken) (there
were conscience clauses hiding in there some-
where) (we'd withdrawn our claws) (we were
not making ticking noises on a staircase) (we
were noiseless) (you could brush up against us)
(we'd filed our barbs off) (it was slippery
on the boulders all along the creekbed) (there
was nothing to hold onto) (we threw you a life-
line) (but it wasn't tied to anything we knew of)

replacements

(not the real one) (another one) (a counter-
feit) (a good one) (worth more than the other one)
(a comment) (a running commentary) (it has to be
running on something) (hope it's not wet caliche)
(they're going to Greece to run an original mara-
thon) (not the first one) (it would take them too
long to get there) (they wouldn't be dressed right)
(they wouldn't know what anyone was saying) (as if
they were stand-ins standing in the wrong movie)

(they'd have to find a toga-stand and another
kind of money) (they'd need to find a money ex-
change) (they'd have to talk with their hands)
(they'd have to appeal to the gods) (there were
plenty of them to appeal to) (they corresponded
with everything) (twig god) (nail of the dog god)
(gold leaf god) (good enough god) (burning log god)
(burrowing insect god) (upperlip god) (god on the run
god) (feather after falling god) (good grip god)

(god-awful god) (good to go god) (jealous god) (god
on the make god) (blowing smoke through its nose
god) (god of clutter) (god of one thing leading to
another) (penny for your thoughts god) (persistent
god) (slightly annoying god) (a dogging you god)
(god of calisthenics) (of repetitive motions)
(makeshift god) (waiting in the wings god) (left
at the altar god) (left behind at the beginning
of the marathon) (they'd missed the starting

torches) (they felt awful then) (they felt like
underachievers) (and they'd traveled so far back
in time to get there) (they'd had to pass through
so much security) (all of their weapons had been
confiscated) (they couldn't even file their own
nails) (they couldn't sharpen their pencils) (a
feather could tip them over) (a quill could)
(then they'd be tattooed with inkspots) (they'd
have more quirks than they knew what to do with)

(they needed a station break) (they needed a
pause) (they were like sitting ducks) (they were
babes in the woods) (they were stationary station-
ery) (there were no strong gusty winds there)
(there were no streets to be blown down) (there
were no airshafts to live in) (they'd get step-
ped on) (they'd be covered with footprints) (they
were acting like doormats) (play-acting in some-
body else's play) (they'd been two-timed) (they

were ready for log-rolling) (they were lumber-
jacks) (it was a sport) (it was logical) (and a
pastime) (that is specious reasoning) (we needed
new representatives) (our proxies were not on our
side) (we were weightless) (from deep down in a
caldera you could barely hear us murmuring) (we
were under their radar) (we couldn't be kept in
their logs) (we were playing possums) (we were
looking around in some sleepscapes) (we were like

burrowing insects) (we were divergent metallic
wood-boring beetles) (it was our hideout) (that's
where we hid our hides) (we were smugglers then)
(we were bootleggers) (we were special skullduggery
agents) (it was a masquerade) (we needed good dis-
guises) (we needed a carnival) (we needed some
gambling houses) (there'd be shills there) (and
lots of little old ladies) (and hookers & bookies)
(and lots of our very own blood relatives) (they'd

be all monogrammed) (they'd be programmed to find
us) (we'd be their long lost everything) (they'd
want to take us back to their caves with them)
(they'd want to haul out all the old recipes)
(rev up all the home movies) (dust off a ton of
dust off some of their favorite stories) (we'd
never get out of there) (we'd have been kidnapped)
(we'd suddenly become very sleepy) (we'd be nar-
coleptics) (we'd smell like orange blossoms)

(they'd tie our hair up in ribbons) (in poppy-
aughts) (they'd study us in their jacklights)
(they'd bring us along to check on their traps)
(we'd be carrying a bucket of bait) (we'd have
our straw hats back) (we wouldn't have shoes any
more) (we'd be afraid to cross over the cattle-
guard) (where a cougar lived) (we'd go hide
in a haystack) (we'd be like needles) (they'd use
us to mend things) (they'd stand us in pincushions)

A crew of reinforcements
In mystery and a deep line

(out from an eternity over which double
doors of an elevator are shutting) (you inside it)
(it is so slowly closing) (there's only one
way for it to be going) (and the tail of your
raincoat can get caught in it) (so dappled it
is from where you just had been running) (and
its steel panel has braille on it) (so you
touch it) (you look at it while the elevator's
doors are still closing) (until there's nothing

but one long seam showing) (like a seam laid
down a length of leg by a stocking) (that's
what we were doing) (we were throwing out thou-
sands of fish for a river) (we were inside a
warehouse backing around a corner on a forklift)
(we were emitting a steady backing-up warning)
(someone else was doing the steering) (it was
dark inside where we were waiting to be shipped
somewhere) (to be opened) (to serve a purpose)

(to seek our destiny) (as if we were employed
by nature) (we were foils then) (we made other
foils look even better) (we stuck to thin sheets
of glass to make mirrors) (we were not allowed
to stand straight in front of one) (we stood to
the side see over our shoulders) (then we broke
them) (and threw them all into a river) (that was
one of their superstitions) (they passed it down
to us) (it made walking on a riverbed dangerous)

(so from different angles water surfaces would
shimmer) (and you could be mesmerized) (and have
your thoughts go different places) (over where
their flags said they'd come from) (you knew where
they were going) (straight to the wharf) (to the
why) (to the whatsoever) (where the forklifts wait
to unlead them) (barely knowing what was inside
them) (whether it was alive or dying) (that was
the one whose hull was broken open) (and from out

of it floated thousands of little wooden coffins)
(it was foggy) (there were rats with laser-red eyes
standing on some of them) (it was in technicolor)
(a bucket of blood had been splashed on the face of
the moon) (it was garish) (we had no taste then)
(we were worse than cold biscuits) (we were going
to be given to chickens) (we'd be pecked to death)
(and pretty soon we'd be breakfast) (again) (we
were in some kind of closed circuit) (we had to get

out of there) (the little aforementioned coffins
were too small for us) (they were decoys) (we'd
sink them straight down to the riverbed with us)
(we'd be stuck there) (we might be eaten alive by
what's down there) (and later on someone would
say we were delicious) (we'd been sizzling) (some-
one had battered us) (we were boiling in oil) (we
were heartpoison) (there were warning signs all
over us in those days) (we were warned about every-

thing) (that wasn't good for us) (it twisted
our thoughts around) (like we were strands of
hair in a tornado) (like we were unwilling in-
gredients in an industrial-sized very efficient
blender) (we had to get back to the river) (that's
where our boat was) (that's where we'd left it)
(we'd pick it up and carry it on our shoulders)
(we'd treat it as if it were just a baby)
(we'd rock it to sleep) (we'd hum songs to it)

(we'd nurse it) (then it couldn't be a boat any
longer) (it could be a shark then) (it could be
some kind of intoxicating drink you want to think
through) (it could need your protection) (you
might be the one whose job it is to watch over it)
(we could be nightlights) (we could use barely any
electricity) (we could be starlight) (before there
were constellations) (before we had names we had
nothing to do with) (we were like streets then)

(we were like subdivisions) (we didn't grow up
naturally) (there were too many stakes in us)
(like we were vampires) (until someone splashed
a bucket of water on us) (and our trees started
growing) (fast growing trees not the slow ones)
(not the ones we'd need to take our time with)
(we didn't know what patience was back then)
(we were like bottle rockets) (we were something
a little dangerous children could play with)

land of plenty

(they were the landed gentry) (the never-
neverland bosses) (that was their classroom)
(they learned about class in there) (no one
ever figured out how many there were) (it was
painful) (to watch the doctors of philosophy
theorize about things they'd never be allowed
to see) (they were off in the distance) (from
far away it sounded dimly and with sure reverb-
erations) (like galloping horses) (that is the

sound of creation) (ripsawing through the old
universe) (like when a baby starts breathing)
(no) (don't emote now) (emote has a bad reputa-
tion) (we were embers then) (we were waiting
for someone to stoke us) (our eyes traveled
fast then) (like thousands of little red lasers)
(we'd been emblazoned) (shovels were under us)
(we were being carried away in buckets) (where
were they taking us) (we were too cold by then

to know that) (we couldn't tell the difference)
(they could take us seven thousand miles from
where we started) (we wouldn't know what was hap-
pening) (they could take us across all their
timezones) (we were valued one timezone per per-
son) (we felt very expensive) (as if we ought
to be feeling and thinking with our pricetags in
mind) (as part of the inventory) (so invent some)
(make up a trademark) (take out a patent) (go re-

gister something) (act like a geiger counter)
(go find an earthquake) (take out a birth cer-
tificate) (there's a footprint on it) (we were
nothing but ripplemarks) (sandpipers walked all
over us) (maybe we were godwits) (mud-probers)
(ember-stirrers) (we had sticks in our hands)
(some of the ends of our sticks were burning)
(to scare away flying roaches) (to write on our
cavewalls) (to draw something resembling part

of a thought we were having) (and the one we
were following) (it was perfectly still) (it
was going around in a circle) (sort of a circle)
(it was circling while it was going) (it was
tumbling while it was at it) (our gyroscopes
were on red alert) (they were almost over-loaded)
(we couldn't tell up from down) (we were in an
upside down mineshaft) (we were in a library)
(with its anti-gravity drive going topspeed)

(books were flying every which way) (worse
than roaches) (we needed our anti-torque rotors)
(roaches have been around forever) (you were
the one wearing a gold collar) (you were the one
with a gold tooth to spare) (you were the one
with a gravely wrinkled forehead) (it marked
how you thought about everything) (as if you
were born worried) (which seems a sensible be-
ginning) (given all we've been through) (and

where we will certainly end up) (our riot-acts
were being read to us) (then we were very small
children) (it was our bedtime) (a kind of amnesia
had set in) (the way it feels to be watching some-
one sleeping) (as if they were present) (by means
of your mind) (that wouldn't be what they were
thinking) (they'd be dreaming of other things)
(we could be in their dreams without knowing so)
(we could be all tangled up in their nightmares)

(there's no free will in there) (no choices for
nothing) (so all of the consequences are different)
(and then you wake up) (you don't have any shoes
on) (you are barefoot) (while you were sleeping
they walked away on their own) (that's why you see
them now and then just lying on the side of a
highway) (they are roadkill) (that creates little
leeway) (there's multiplication and division)
(that's a subdivision) (they name the streets

after their children) (we're in ragdom) (we're
in the broken districts) (we're in tractdom)
(there's not much elbowroom in there) (we're in
doomtown) (it's the place they put their children
to make them be just like them) (you can hear them
crying) (you can hear them whimpering) (that's the
way they like them) (they torture them down into
exhaustion) (they're gone) (they're leaving) (they're
not coming back) (then they give them their names)

hydrotaxis

(you'll find them in cemeteries) (with little
bits of white gravel scattered over their faces)
(with too much glare in bright sunlight) (and
old iron bedframes for gravemarkers) (out in the
middle of nowhere) (where winds start and go back
to) (close near a levee and lower) (you can see
inside their bricks are loose) (you can
lift bricks away from their walls) (and look in)
(there was nothing to see) (it was always too

dark in there) (ants were always leaving from
inside their corners) (carrying polite requests
on their backs) (bringing out the news from the
other world) (remaining rapturously fixed on their
missions) (hauling back into daylight all the things
they were saying) (one letter at a time) (not even
all of a whole one) (it was an endless procession)
(they are the most silent messengers) (they work-
ed under very strict orders) (they were taking

things down to the river) (a barge was waiting
to be loaded) (there was nobody on it) (it was
tied by a rope to a willow) (so an ant would have
a way to get there) (leave what it was carrying)
(and go back to where it came from) (we waited
past midnight) (until all the fish were sleep-
ing) (you kept your knife wrapped in a blanket)
(we didn't want any moonlight flashes) (birds
weren't doing anything) (but there were some

crickets) (intermittent ones) (saluting one
another) (like when I sneeze and you say god
bless you) (as if they were staying in touch
with one another over very long distances)
(letting each other know all their whereabouts)
(describing the range of their territories)
(say you're a mapmaker) (show them your owl
eyes) (show them your contours) (give them
one of your business cards) (sell them some

maps at a discount) (throw in one for free)
(with everything wrong on it) (give them your
lantern) (point them in some direction) (say
you don't want their money) (tell them their
money's no good where you are) (then get back
to your drawing) (wait until you no longer can
hear their footsteps) (they will be far out of
earshot) (we can tell each other what we are
thinking) (or we can sit here in silence)

(as if we were armed with patience) (covered
with ataraxia) (all tranquil) (as if we were
still pools) (as if water lilies were floating
on us) (and muskrats nowhere near us) (and no
one skipping rocks on us) (and nobody throwing
into us) (things they no longer wanted) (some-
thing they didn't want anyone else to see any-
more) (something they needed to hide) (some-
thing that hurt them) (something they hurt some-

one else with) (it doesn't seem we can
have that much room in us) (we'd have to be
cavernous) (we'd have more still pools in us)
(and blind fish would swim in us) (we would
have twilight zones) (bats would live in us)
(people would turn us into tourist attractions)
(people would get married in us) (they'd tell
the same story over and over) (like some kind
of dripping water torture) (until it made their

children crazy) (there would be mineral deposits
on them) (slowly over the course of millennia)
(they would turn into something different) (people
would tell them they looked like knifeblades) (they
would have to sit there straight-faced) (with
their bladed eyes unblinking) (and it would be
dark where they were) (and you could hear some
muffled sobbing) (and someone would have burst
into tears) (and there wouldn't be any sniveling)

(it's hard to weep for a knifeblade) (someone's wept
for one before) (not in these circumstances)
(we don't know what these circumstances are)
(we don't know who we are) (we have no idea
where we came from) (no wonder we're always looking
for something) (as if we had very bad memories)
(as if memory weren't something we made up)
(we were infinitesimally small bits of a
story) (little missiles stonecarvers look away from)

. . . it is the shadow building that counts

(but then later on) (later was better then)
(it was the longest known snake in the world)
(it was a girl) (she had a headboard) (music
came out of it) (from far away from her) (she
could barely hear it) (it showed her how to
listen) (she wanted to pay attention) (she had
to learn to not move then) (to not let any winds
in) (to be a very small boat in a soupbowl)
(in the backcorner of the highest shelf in a

cupboard) (there would be plenty of slacktime)
(she'd have to stay with her anchor down)
(like floating for good where no water is)
(going a little swayback) (but the other way
around) (she was almost something to trace on)
(she was tracing paper) (we could put her over
something) (we could see through her) (she work-
ed like our eyes work) (she was a peephole)
(nobody could see us when we stood inside

looking out of her) (listening for noises)
(listening for footsteps) (keeping our lids on)
(playing dead to the world) (as if silencers
had been attached to all of us) (as if we were
dangerous) (we were rusty razors then) (we left
stains on their porcelain) (we left
our marks on their bathtubs) (someone was always
coming to scrub us away) (and then forgetting about
us until the next time) (there were more important

things on the horizon) (we were not a part of
their strategy) (we weren't on the agenda)
(our names weren't in their addressbooks)
(they didn't need to know what our names were)
(all they needed to know was whether we were
able-bodied or not) (to see if we could read
well enough to take orders) (and later on they
could put some of our names on their monuments)
(to convince themselves they really loved us)

(and that their cause had been righteous) (you
be Saint Ignatius Loyola then) (go found a so-
ciety) (sigh so many times you start a new lang-
uage) (start with a clean slate) (listen to a
hard rain falling on it straight through a couple
of dozen midnights) (translate that into some-
thing) (run it through several translation sta-
tions) (of the cross smothered in incense) (of
its song sung through latin) (not by grown-ups)

(only children who don't understand the words
can be singing it) (as if they really mean it)
(as if it frightens them when they feel it)
(and a feeling they wanted to run away from)
(is living inside them) (that's when a breeze
blows a curtain too close to a candleflame)
(that's when what's smoldering turns into some-
thing different) (go ask St. Augustine) (after
he's believed he's tried all of the possible

combinations) (and was making himself a little
crazy) (when his attention shifted) (he changed
his mind) (he altered his position) (he became
single-minded) (like a bullet) (*the means by which*)
(*they cease to be*) (*what they had been*) (*and be-*
gin) (*to be what*) (*they have not been*) (the result
of the rapping) (of spirits) (a sort of wash and
wear tweaking) (a snatch and a wrench and a hush)
(a bush and a stench and a watch) (a catch and a

bench and a lush) (a team-player) (no fly-by-
night) (a good thistle whacker) (oil of hitches)
(oil of plucking) (oil of pure analysis) (good
grade stuff) (you buy it from school houses) (they
give you it) (it's what they've got to give)
(we can unburden them of some) (we can be camels)
(we can go without anything to drink for a long
time) (then we'll come upon an oasis) (a pretty
mirage one) (we'll be sleeping on blankets under

datepalms) (a girl will be combing her long hair)
(her black hair) (she'll be combing her thoughts
over her shoulder) (her head will be empty) (her
eyes will be open) (she doesn't look as if she can
see us) (she'll be combing her memories down into
blue water) (where the moon is) (where just a few
stars are hiding) (she'll be combing her hair
for a long time) (we can turn into sand now)
(we can turn into water) (later on) (water)

autocracy

(its effects wouldn't happen until later)
(down the road) (not until long after) (not
close) (not by a long shot) (a keen caustic
sniper) (we are doing its aftermath) (we're
drowning in it) (with chains on) (our ankles)
(if you open that door) (and go over its thresh-
old) (with enough sufficient) (to begin to)
(cause something to happen) (no one will find
you) (no one will be there) (the place will

be empty) (you'll be worth a few pennies)
(you'll be crushed) (broken to bits) (mixed
with) (messed with) (you'll be in one of their)
(redemption centers) (ants will like you)
(rats will) (live on what was inside us) (we'll
be still as sticks then) (we'll go very)
(grow very) (quiet) (it sounds as if) (someone
is coming) (you can hear their hoofbeats)
(one beat at a time) (as if they were metro-

nomes) (with their own private) (subcurrents)
(something we sensed) (something we seemed)
(to know little) (or nothing) (about) (this
time) (we went stepwise) (as if we were)
(avoiding something) (keeping our heads down)
(avoiding eye contact) (pretending as if)
(we didn't notice) (we were in shock then)
(before we were shockproof) (stunned) (para-
lyzed) (as if we'd been frozen) (saved for

later) (stockpiled) (put in a pillory) (made
out of nothing) (given a curfew) (without
a timeframe) (sentenced to parley) (until we
were threadbare) (we'd lost our street clothes)
(we couldn't be seen in public) (we were like
old straw) (animals had been sleeping on us)
(it was the longest night of the year) (nothing
you can do) (about that) (about this) (you
can do something) (about) (this time we'd be more)

(like a metropolis) (nothing's capital) (no-
thing's homebase) (a farflung parlando sub-
culture) (a little more dimensional) (less
deluded) (there'd be no cant in us) (we wouldn't
be whiners) (all sing-songy) (we wouldn't be
beggars) (no more) (emotional) (extortion) (of
any kind) (no more skull sessions) (contests)
(of foregone conclusions) (too many split-
ends) (the stakes would be higher) (there'd

be no heads stuck up on them) (back then we
were headless) (and heartless) (filled with
cunning) (and courage) (we were monsters then)
(we constructed our own) (private labyrinths)
(we carried them with us) (wherever) (wind
blew us) (seeds of malcontent) (seeds of illu-
sion) (you could order us) (from catalogs) (in
the dead) (of winter) (we were dormant then)
(we were sleeping) (as if we were sleeping syl-

lables) (nothing had stressed us) (no one
had written) (what we were made of) (all over
us) (our nerves) (were not raw steel then)
(what we hid) (in our hearts) (no one could
see then) (we hadn't been traded) (no one
was trying to buy us) (to feed their families)
(to put food on the table) (to bring home)
(the bacon) (it's hard to) (stomach that) (make
it believable) (we were pigseeds then) (something

new on the news stand) (nobody'd buy that)
(right out of the tabloids) (we could see the
headlines) (where our brows had been knit)
(we worried) (too) (we got) (everything) (back-
wards) (we worried because) (we had to) (on
account of) (circumstances) (poor repair) (dis-
repair) (shabby) (rituals) (broken railings)
(to hold on to) (rotten floorboards) (to hide
things beneath) (someone will find everything)

(no matter) (where you put it) (and tell you)
(all about it) (demand you believe) (everything
as they say so) (threaten to) (defeat you)
(slap you) (silly) (part of their parlance)
(patrilinear) (ceremonies of pain) (on whose) (be-
half) (they say raid now) (act like a rampage)
(salute on the ramparts) (pay homage) (pay with)
(your lives) (put your life) (on the line)
(not) (your) (personal) (private) (autonomy)

unselfconscious

(having been born) (having been at one time a
baby) (unable to do much) (by way of helping
one's self) (at the mercy of) (those around you)
(to look after you) (to keep an eye on you) (to
figure out) (what it is you want now) (you couldn't
want much) (you hadn't a clue) (what was much past
your cradle) (those around you) (came and went out of
nowhere) (they trailed noises behind them) (sounds
came before them) (sometimes they would move you)

(to be more content) (or less lonely) (though
lonely wouldn't have been what you called it) (con-
cepts would come later) (far into your future) (there)
(would be cauldrons of concepts) (would be landscapes
of notions) (there would be half a mind to) (do one
thing) (you could listen) (to music) (some of them
who would sing to no one else) (would sing to you)
(you made them sound better) (it was very quiet singing)
(an audience of just one baby) (a captured audience)

(if ever there was one) (gradually you incrementally
did more things) (added to your repertoire) (very
useful abilities) (randomly rolling around) (catching
on to what fingers can do) (kicking for different reasons)
(using your knees) (in remarkably brilliant ways) (pride
seemed to be dawning on you) (pleasure was becoming more
complicated) (you were beginning to get somewhere) (you
could move yourself) (most of all toward something) (to
back away from) (hadn't seemed to dawn on you at

this time) (to crawl in reverse) (required a new
skillset) (it took immense concentration) (it wasn't
something you could automatically do) (you'd have
to think about it) (meanwhile you could drop things)
(it was a very powerful dropping) (and eventually
you could hurl and fling) (in an effort to keep things)
(moving) (you seemed offended) (when undropping didn't
appear to be on the agenda) (when something couldn't
unhurl itself in your direction) (this helped you

want to start a conversation) (about how it's pos-
sible to make anything happen) (it gave you an in-
centive) (to find ways to make yourself understood)
(they didn't understand you) (it was hard to follow
your expressions sometimes) (so you needed to find
how to get what you wanted) (your strategies were
very limited) (nevertheless) (you were sizing up
your surroundings) (you were noticing) (you were not
putting two and two together yet) (that would come

later) (after you were standing) (up to be counted)
(you were changing the way) (you related to things)
(a new boldness set in) (you were building up courage)
(sometimes you were adamantly decisive) (kind of stub-
born) (even willful) (you were waiting for something)
(to be more satisfying) (you wouldn't have called it
that) (you wanted to be lost in what you were doing)
(you didn't want to think about it) (things thought
through you at this time) (you weren't fully in charge

of what you were thinking) (you never would be)
(or you'd be reduced to unthinking) (which is some-
thing that rarely happens) (you'd gotten to the
point) (where you could do everything backwards)
(you were fairly certain) (of how to turn a corner)
(without reeling over) (you were adding variation
to your straight lines) (for a while this induced
trances of spinning) (for its own sake) (because
you were drilling a well of what you were doing)

(you were tunneling) (that's what snow was good for)
(you were finding things) (to build with) (soon you
were building cities with everything cities have in
them) (you were populating) (your cities of building)
(with a new cast of characters) (you didn't seem to
live in the same world you used to) (you were busy)
(there were marriages, doctors, fires, places to buy
things, funerals, a few major catastrophes, schools,
prayerplaces, roads to build, railroads, bridges, animals

were very good substitute humans) (in general you favored
them) (with better qualities) (only the best for them)
(though you could be brutal) (you would have to be) (if
you weren't) (you'd have an awfully one-dimensional city)
(no vicissitudes) (no brutal awakenings) (not much of a
story) (you were in favor) (of finding out everything)
(no matter) (the consequences) (were never stable) (you
were agile by now) (you could be leading several parallel
lives) (always) (you were the last thing) (you thought of)

. . . which I began as a secret diary and which has
become a confession

(scree was) (the pushed in knitted back)
(pull-string what's that tight) (thing with
no father on) (it jumped back) (it went with)
(no haircut) (for its whole life) (with too
much old hair on) (cold as lace) (rock liquid)
(choppy rice) (unfurled birds) (in some blue
notches) (some gone away stitches) (runaways)
(road hitters) (time snackers) (crease wasters)
(crested wavers) (old time time savers) (box

lovers) (squeeze tight) (toe bearers) (face
gazers) (if-you-can-wanters) (wind parters)
(inch shavers) (everything you didn't do takers)
(no place you ever went it ever went elsewheres)
(time passers) (amalgamation weavers) (throat
catchers) (take away take away takers) (mix
mixers) (backgrounders) (watch and see keepers)
(look long and hard framers) (here and now hear-
ers) (flock flockers) (band banders) (if & when

finders) (spot notchers) (mudslingers) (deck
stackers) (premeditated riggers) (agenda swap-
pers) (backroom spurners) (fatalists) (wild
card snappers) (go to pieces wiggers) (unglued)
(not attached to anything simmering) (discontin-
uous choreline) (almost numb drum) (slow sad
blisters) (soul sifters) (see how they run
keepers) (up and down mounters) (catch as catch
can zippers) (into the night creepers) (where

to go drifters) (down and out lifters) (end
of the road settlers) (last one for miles
shoppers) (head twisters) (what iffers) (your
place or mine shakers) (salt in a wound wound-
ers) (your money or your lifesavers) (your
money and your life bandits) (what happens
then throwers) (what next slingers) (keep it
to yourself canners) (out the door testers)
(heads on straight senders) (eyes saying it

all whispers) (wanting for something sweeter)
(wanting for something clearer) (wishing for
something disappearing) (watching it flicker
away) (fall through your fingers) (past under-
standing) (out of reach) (unavailable) (dis-
regarded) (ignored) (unseen) (unimagined)
(so you turn your back on it) (as if it were
some kind of skillet) (you turn yourself over
and into something different) (you turn in on

yourself) (you turn on your own set of cir-
cumstances) (a little too hot) (a little too
dizzy) (like a horn on an animal's head)
(that's taken a very wrong turn) (that's headed in
the wrong direction) (that's going back inside
where it came from) (and nothing can stop it)
(it has a mind of its own) (that's extremely
fatalistic) (too finalized) (too gloom beat)
(too done on all sides) (so send it back where

it came from) (let someone else's mind turn
it over) (and you run for cover) (you take
yourself out of harm's way) (out of harm's
way) (you have more time there to slow down)
(not get slapped on the fast track) (never
knowing what hit you) (blind-sided) (blind-
folded and spun around until you're stag-
gering) (it's just a game kids play in twi-
light) (now you go find them) (they'll make

funny noises to let you hear where they are)
(you can lurch around after them) (or you can
just stand there) (you can look like blind
justice) (you can pretend you're holding a
pair of scales in your right hand) (or you
can take off your blindfold) (you can see
what it's made of) (you might recognize where
it came from) (a worn-out shirt someone's
sent to a ragbin) (a cribsheet that's been

consigned to history) (as we say in the stories)
(a plain white handkerchief) (you can wave it
up in the air) (you can put your scales down)
(or you can use your left hand) (you aren't
surrendering) (you're suggesting) (you're not
suggesting anything's over) (you're proposing
an end to hostilities) (a kind of peace-offer-
ing) (or you can fold your flag until it's small
enough to put in your pocket) (or you can drop it)

self-conscious

(now and then now) (all of the surfaces of every-
thing) (someone had gone around re-surfacing) (in-
terjecting every surface with things reflecting)
(you began to notice this in bits and pieces) (not
everything) (held your attention) (was not monolithic)
(you didn't will this to happen) (inch by inch) (al-
most before you knew it) (you'd catch a glimpse of
yourself) (away from where you were) (you were in
grasses) (you could see yourself) (in treetrunks)

(in your shoes you'd positioned for take-off) (in
bowls of hot soup intoxicating a table) (in and it
awed you) (a pencil you could see your hand holding)
(in and you were beguiled) (with how you looked in
the night sky) (in and it shook you) (it shook your
foundation) (a part of a building you'd never thought
about) (was suddenly a matter of urgent attention)
(if there was one thing) (you'd overlooked) (there
must be infinite others) (you couldn't hide) (from

yourself) (any longer) (for the first time) (you could
talk to yourself) (in earnest) (you were becoming
your own correspondent) (you corresponded) (was it to)
(is it with) (everything had something to tell you)
(about yourself) (you could hear yourself talking)
(you recognized what you were doing) (in and you could
be paralyzed) (taking measure of yourself) (against the
rampantly advancing multiplications) (you could see
coming into view) (your point of view was re-positioning)

(you had a job to do now) (you could be dumb-
founded) (you turned out to be your own mirror
image) (no one had asked you) (you hadn't volunteered)
(for the assignment) (self-denial didn't seem to be)
(one of the options) (self-control was way too dra-
conian) (that was no way to treat) (a stranger) (some-
one new to you) (from not from where you're from)
(with different customs) (a history) (ways of knowing
different from your ways) (you were in the early

stages) (of getting acquainted) (it was possible)
(for there to be misunderstandings) (you seemed to
want to get to know one another) (deeply) (you
wanted to make a good impression) (on one another)
(you could trade valuable information) (you noticed)
(what a glance could make happen) (what a tone of
voice could accomplish) (you studied one another's
speech patterns) (you could mock one another when
you wanted) (you were fairly synchronized) (most of

the time) (you could be made uncomfortable) (by your
own shadow) (what if your shadow) (turned out to be
your rival) (hounding you) (dogging you) (never letting
you out of its sight) (making you watch your back)
(questioning your every move) (keeping you on a short
leash) (eyeing you with suspicion) (questioning your
motives) (never letting you) (forget what you're doing)
(get lost in something you want to lose yourself) (in)
(causing you great aggravation) (that involuntary self-

shadowing contraption) (you would have to make
peace with) (deflect or absorb it) (or else) (you'd
end up having) (your best conversations) (all one-
sided) (you end up liking to listen to yourself most)
(you'd wind up) (you could really get wound up) (prac-
tically frozen) (you'd always be fearing) (what anyone
else thought of you) (in the eyes of another)
(you looked for signs) (of how you were doing) (of
approval) (which you were afraid) (was not forthcoming)

(your interpretations were shaded) (deep in self-
doubt) (deep in self-castigation) (deep in drop to
your knees howling in drowning self-incrimination)
(you needed some self-effacement lotion) (some self-
forgetful strong medicine) (which is easy enough)
(to find on any street corner) (reasons for abandon)
(ment) (of self-consciousness) (what would you trade
to be self-forgetful) (you will have to commit to self-
treasonous acts) (for which you can punish yourself)

(or deny them altogether) (blame someone else) (make
up an alibi) (exercise your criminal mind) (sheer)
(nerve) (you were making yourself overly overly ner-
vous) (paying yourself too much attention) (scruti-
nizing) (giving yourself a hard time) (you were your
own self-styled jurisdiction) (your own) (monomaniac)
(wind blew for you) (alone) (rivers ran for your ex-
clusive observation) (there were still others around
you) (sometimes in awe) (beside your strenuous metamorphosis)

There are many people who come back

(might as well be ironing) (a complicated
blouse) (or sorting seeds) (you could be
watching) (I could be walking) (in a daze)
(in a cemetery) (scattered in the woods)
(you could be in there) (hiding) (it would
be just as well) (to be unstitching thread)
(from a perfectly hand-stitched hem) (count-
ing) (something that doesn't) (need to be
counted) (combing through things) (needing

no combing) (untangling) (something already
untangled) (we could be in a boat then) (we
would have been fishing) (we'd be in a swamp
there) (in one of its channels) (with cypress
trees everywhere around us) (it would be
almost dusk now) (we'd be surrounded) (by
owls) (they'd be looking) (as if they couldn't
see us) (that's when our line broke) (we had
to leave it) (we couldn't take it with us)

(we left it behind) (it was abandoned) (for-
gotten) (no use to us anymore) (an obstacle)
(a barricade) (a battery) (of too many ques-
tions) (we didn't tell them) (where we were
sleeping) (what we were doing) (we didn't say)
(what they wanted to hear) (we kept our own
counsel) (we unlearned their language) (we
turned off our recognition meters) (we went
back to zero) (before that) (we were negative

numbers) (we were useful) (we were a way
around) (very many contradictions) (we were
like circles) (we were overlapping) (one
another) (we were looking for similarities)
(wherever we looked) (we would find them)
(saying good-bye) (in the morning) (snow
would be all over everything) (all they'd
leave were their footprints) (wind would
blow them away) (in fine smoking sheets

over highways) (in sandsmoke moving
over some beachheads) (we would be beach-
combers then) (we would be beachdrift)
(we would stick with the contours) (not to
disturb) (what we found there) (not to
erode anything) (not to damage) (what
hasn't been damaged) (any more than it's
already been) (you go undamage something
then) (unbreak it) (unscathe it) (unhex it)

(uncross it) (unharm it) (undemolish some-
thing) (make a countermove) (deploy some-
thing) (makeshift) (something uncertain)
(without any strategies) (no trying to
outmaneuver anything) (without second guess-
ing) (go restore something) (reforest some-
thing) (remind yourself) (have your own
thoughts) (not someone else's) (remind your-
self) (where you stored something) (you might

want to find again) (to give it to someone)
(you might want to keep for later) (not
something) (you go to bazaars for) (not
something) (you find on a rack) (not some-
thing) (you see in a catalog) (as though
through a dim light darkly) (in the pages)
(over the loudspeakers) (inside a seed
catalog) (where you can find complicated
blouses) (and gadgets) (good old time-

savers) (logic monsters) (economical grip-
pers) (rules) (they say we should go by)
(requirements) (things we must have) (as if
that were possible) (who could know so)
(there's nothing to base it on) (it has no
baseline) (nothing to stand on) (no balls)
(to go in or out or over it) (we were near
a very large grandstand) (a whip-cracking
stadium) (a people-pouncing mob was in there)

(they were watching fireworks) (exploding
over and above them) (they were busy) (cel-
ebrating some ancient victory) (their team
was winning) (we were watching) (a great
celebration) (a triumph) (a vindication)
(a mandate) (a result) (of their tenacious
certainty) (they were like giants then)
(we were like seedlings) (we'd just barely
started breathing) (our eyes weren't even open)

nothing matches

(strike nowhere) (sticks) (versus) (no) (flash)
(lights) (out) (deferred) (underratcheted) (static)
(to hear) (static to wear) (standard) (Ah) (my
little clumsy) (tipsy) (gypsy) (versus) (your)
(giant) (silent) (sober) (oaktree) (cancelled)
(no) (feast) (no) (plenty) (famine) (standard)
(Oh) (you) (flippy) (see-saw) (circle) (circus)
(versus) (you) (died-in-the-rope) (jumping) (rodeo)
(torpedo) (cancelled) (you) (are) (my) (cause)

(my stick) (stirring) (watertap) (good) (you)
(are not a greasetrap) (versus) (you) (are a
very fine waterglass) (lips) (like you) (leave)
(evidence) (everywhere all around them) (you
have bothered) (been bothered) (been brothered)
(because) (you were thinking about knowing nothing)
(about your future) (not even) (tomorrow) (not to
mention) (where) (you might be living) (we could
hear) (in your voice) (somehow) (this made you)

(very happy) (almost) (thrilled) (you) (you)
(turned) (a corner) (good) (for your axles)
(you) (have) (very) (fine) (ankles) (snakes)
(don't) (really) (bother) (you) (snakes) (don't)
(have) (ankles) (deferred) (just four letters)
(next) (to) (on top) (of) (one another) (standard)
(no) (consensus) (we are all in agreement) (de-
ferred) (cancelled) (postponed) (smashed to the
ground) (undeliverable) (letters) (interchange-

able) (capable) (uncapsized) (very zippered)
(we) (ask) (very much) (very many) (of) (one)
(another) (we) (live on) (very) (many) (levels)
(to) (strike) (a balance) (deferred) (sometimes)
(determined) (it was) (just the way) (something)
(turned out) (in) (retrospect) (versus) (in order)
(for) (something) (to) (happen) (someone) (or)
(something) (has) (to) (do) (something) (stand-
ard) (procedure) (standard) (practice) (stand-

ard) (hard) (going) (going) (to) (sleep) (as oft-
en as) (possible) (in) (order) (to) (wake-up)
(in case) (this time) (everything) (will) (be)
(otherwise) (and) (you) (will) (feel) (good) (a-
gain) (standard) (deviations) (delivered) (un-
rivalled) ("this lake has a peculiar shape")
(we) (are) (just beginning) (to scratch) (the
surface) (sgrafitto) (like) (in) (gradeschool)
(smell of crayons) (deferred) (almost) (a square

deal) (versus) (lilies you hear) (by a lake-
side) (versus) (it looks) (to) (me) (like) (a)
(stand-off) (versus) (try not) (to be so) (stand-
offish) (versus) (there were no) (standards of
living) (left) (anywhere) (standing) (next to)
(someone) (or something) (you) (want to) (stand)
(by) (more) (will be) (coming later) (shades and
shadows) (can give a) (building) (more) (charac-
ter) (versus) ("that is a fine sipid lakewater")

("let me fill your waterglass") ("allow me to")
(show them your stanchions) (ask them how they
got to be) (so standardized) (one's left with)
(a fighting chance) (never) (to be recognized)
(known by) (one's profile) (a real snow stopper)
(a snow fence) (a windbreak) (a true shelterbelt)
("so we're in agreement") (not to) (do anything)
(to untouch) (the bluing) (not to) (do anything)
(versus) (and) (this) (is) (standard) (advice)

(coinciding) (incidental) (implanted) (fast)
(growing) (named after) (their fences) (were
known as) (tumbleweed catchers) (all it takes)
(is one match) (they are) (highly) (inflammable)
(tinderboxes) (standard) (versus) ("the thought
takes a peculiar shape") ("here is your very own
necklace") (when) (your) (neck) (is) (nowhere in
the vicinity) (your neck) (you stuck out) (your
neck) (you carry on) (your expertly) (arranged)

(both) (shoulders) (Ah) (versus) ("they were match-
makers") (deferred) ("a match made") (you know
where) (it will take a very long time to get here)
(through a snowstorm) (we can watch) (the long
string) (of cancellations) (postponements) (dis-
asters) (disappointments) (we cancelled) (and
kept) (many) (appointments) (with gusto!) (with
fervor!) (now we were) (impassioned necklaces)
(versus) ("let me refill your already full waterglass")

overlapping silences

(stack of suitcases) (over in a corner of a
closet's floor) (stack of boxes) (folded sweat-
ers) (shirts & jackets on well-spaced hangers)
(half a dozen) (empty blouses) (pairs of shoes
and boots and slippers) (one wide black woven
belt looped over two nails) (a paper sack filled
with papers) (we opened suitcases) (they
were empty) (we shook boxes) (nothing hap-
pened) (we checked pockets) (looking for

evidence) (we found nothing) (it was contagious)
(we rummaged) (through sacks) (filled with
records of business) (transactions) (there was
nothing) (suspicious) (nothing) (to write home
about) (airline tickets) (parking & dinner re-
ceipts) (scratches in margins) (we couldn't de-
cipher) (we understood nothing) (we had nothing
to go on) (you said we'd find something) (we'd
figure it out) (notice something unnoticed)

(remember something) (in retrospect) (in abso-
lute silence) (we'd taken our shoes off) (the
floorboards were icecold) (none of the windows)
(were open) (we could hear one another) (breathing)
(we moved very slowly) (so no one could find us)
(the place was empty) (it was filled) (with their
belongings) (as if they'd ejected) (they left
empty-handed) (they took nothing with them)
(they weren't coming back here) (they'd never

find us) (we weren't what) (they were looking
for) (not on their agenda) (outside of their
roadblocks) (under their radar) (we didn't fit
the descriptions) (we had too much skin on) (our
fingers did too many things) (we went around with
overly individual faces) (it was too confusing)
(that's why they left us) (they'd done all they
could) (they'd tried everything) (we wouldn't
listen) (we couldn't hear them) (there was too

much interference) (no volume) (we were always
out of earshot) (they were talking with one another)
(about how hard it was) (to tame us) (we wouldn't
sit still) (to listen) (they were telling one another
stories) (about where they came from) (who they
belonged to) (this was just a little temporary
interruption) (a small sidetrip) (a mere dogleg)
(a little bit of dogdom) (to drift in and out of)
(to drift far away from) (to never look back at)

(in some of their stories) (you look back) (you
lose everything) (you turn into a saltlick) (&
animals gather around you) (you become the center
of attention) (a dangerous place to be found in)
(there wasn't any such thing) (as a hunting season)
(it was a year-round occupation) (it was always
open season) (you could never let your guard down)
(they were very hungry hunters) (good trackers)
(crackshots) (skillful strategists) (they knew

all your habits) (right where to find you)
(where you'd come back to) (they were sign
readers) (twig thinkers) (trail combers)
(one of them shot your mother) (your father)
(your whole family) (we were skins then) (we
were stew) (we were rugs) (our racks looked
good on their chimneys) (we were trophies)
(we were guardians) (we were amulets) (against
the doldrums) (they were attitudinarians)

(it was exhausting) (they were very adaptive)
(we couldn't keep up with them) (for which
we were lucky) (they were in such a big hurry)
(to keep) (an appointment) (with destiny)
(to get where they were going) (they were
hellbent) (they were glory bound) (we were
blurs in their world) (we were chalkmarks)
(we were like meteors) (when we entered their
atmosphere) (that was the end of us) (meanwhile

bets were placed on us) (superstitions attached
to us) (we were wish buckets) (means to an
end) (peripheral occasions) (we showed up)
(when no one was looking) (we came out of no-
where) (that's where we'd been hiding) (we
were put there) (we had no where else to be then)
(we were waiting) (we were just following orders)
(we were like empty boxes) (stacked one on top of
the other) (waiting for someone to shake us)

and at that moment I heard some comforting words. Words.

(either way or not) (neither before nor aft-
er) (neither you nor I) (but not only us)
(but also them and their kin) (we couldn't
follow them) (we couldn't find a corridor)
(that hadn't been sealed off) (all of the
light switches were broken) (every window
was boarded up) (as if a hurricane were in
the forecast) (you could tell how the air
was coming from a long way off) (all the while

you were waiting) (you were filling up bottles
with water) (fashioning a collection of food
stock) (searching for batteries of many dif-
ferent sizes) (either it was going to hit hard
or it was not) (either you stayed put or you
left for elsewhere) (you gathered up some things)
(you didn't like leaving) (behind some things)
(there were other things behind everything) (you were
rethinking) (re-evaluating) (changing your mind

about everything) (it was a very low pressure
situation) (all of the barometers were falling)
(they fell the way night falls) (when you aren't
looking) (is when almost everything happens)
(when someone builds a throne of human skulls)
(is a very direct statement about someone's posi-
tion) (in relation to what someone stands for)
(and is willing to make public) (& stand by)
(and to try to go as far as possible away from)

(to be evacuees) (always leaving) (never
having) (neither having a choice) (nor able
to choose) (we were like schools of fish
caught up in the waterspouts) (we weren't swim-
ming) (there was no lazy day in summer) (it
was one lousy picnic) (it was worse than that)
(we were out of our water) (we were in over
our heads) (we'd lost our gills) (our lungs
were over-loaded) (we were smothering) (we

wanted out of there) (we were approaching
a cutoff) (some of our relatives were from
there) (we'd hit the hinterlands) (we were
circling the outskirts) (we were like neck-
laces) (made of mercury) (we were almost out
of bounds) (at escape velocity) (almost mach
seven) (we were trespassing) (like sin) (we
were in the wrong airspace) (we could be
paying guests there) (we could be tenant

farmers) (we could be vassals) (we'd have to
turn the clocks back) (we'd have to go in
reverse) (pay homage) (pay tribute) (we'd
have to swear a lot) (swear to be very good
soldiers) (lay down our lives) (as if they
were pitchforks) (as if we were made out of
metal) (and treetrunks) (as if we'd been
made by a blacksmith) (as if we were good
for turning hayrows) (on good days) (when

there wasn't a cloud in the sky) (and you
could see forever) (there was good visibility)
(it was the least common denominator) (a high
pressure system had come through) (everyone
had grown a few inches taller) (their heads
were in the clouds) (it was a tall order)
(we were erring on the high side) (our thinking
was like a very tall building) (we had eleva-
tors in us) (terrible music was in us) (we

were many stories) (stacked up on top of one
another) (with stairwells in us) (that were
like echo chambers) (we were made out of con-
crete then) (we usually didn't have any windows)
(you could get lost in us) (and not know where
you are then) (or what you are doing here) (so
ask someone from upstairs) (someone who's seen
it all) (who knows everything) (who's been there)
(done that) (is like a wind gauge) (like a broken

thermometer) (it couldn't be put back together)
(and it had taken so long to make it) (it was
like the aftermath of a cyclone) (we were down
in the basement) (with the women and children)
(the men were out on the lawns drinking and
smoking) (idly scanning the horizon) (trying
to look as if nothing were happening) (not
betraying any emotion) (the picture of security)
(of conviction) (unerring) (strong) (silent)

For Nine is a number very good and harmonious.

(including) (excluding) (exclusive addresses)
(a weakness for a seamstress) (a fondness of
executives) (a proclivity of dissemblers) (un-
derstanding unstitchers) (taboo inflaters) (chic-
ory beaters) (chicory blooms during harvest) (it
has barely there blue) (gentle cloud physics)
(attached to its petals) (is the rest of what
made them) (grow anywhere season announcers)
(they seem to have) (exclusive rights) (to the

roadway's roadsides) (not particularly) (they
can't be too particular) (they can be isolated
examples) (they can be rare) (more desirable)
(less available) (not so) (expendable) (are those)
(numbers) (who will be sacrificed) (in the name of)
necessity) (loyalty attached to its heraldry)
(is the beast who drove them) (to take up) (sewing)
(for compliments) (you are the most) (significant)
(clew collector) (you have more claws than a clowder

of fatcats) (their claws pale) (in your vicinity)
(as they withdraw them) (to establish credibility)
(it's peaceful) (in the depths) (of the labyrinth)
(there's nothing in there) (that wants to rip your
heart out) (that wants you for supper) (we did the
reconnaissance) (it's safe to go in there) (lay thine
fears aside) (be not thewless) (go thou where we send
thee) (where do we send thee) (one for the little)
(baby) (two to exclusive rights) (to tell the story)

(they say it's the greatest story ever told)
(they have a real rodeo passion for that one)
(who owns the rights) (who claim this is their)
(kingdom) (these are their) (waters) (they own
the clouds) (they have a right) (to the birds)
(they are very bad magpies) (too possessive)
(incorrigible) (with the pride of lions) (they
were having their picture taken) (only two of
them looked) (up) (but not at the camera) (all

of the others were watching the dust) (flee from
where they were walking) (dust was afraid of them)
(dust was sensible) (it had good sense data) (it had been
through the sifters) (had an exclusive education)
(had been given all the advantages) (belonged to the
best conclaves) (all the right references) (the
wrong side of the brain) (was doing all the calcu-
lations) (it would be free) (of impurities) (they
would be essentially ultrapuritanical) (they were so they

were up and running) (refineries) (perverse) (al-
chemical fakeducks) (decoys) (they were hellbent)
(on decoying) (they could fake out the radar) (to be
luring us) (away from the safety) (their safeties
were definitely not on) (but it was uppermost) (in
their minds) (at least) (it looked that way) (to an
amateur) (of being here) (lover of all our rotations)
(just another epicycle) (one more bird's eye) (not
much more than a mildewy dewclaw) (sort of grayblue)

(kind of exclu) (excluded) (the moon's gone)
(sometimes) (we are one stupendous single-minded
shadow) (one hippo shadetree) (the moon's cooling
off around us) (is a moat) (of our own) (making)
(us fill it) (we were good irrigators) (mad good
rivers of weeping) (dispensers) (alligator's tears
were not in us) (we wanted them out of us) (we
could hire some exorcists) (to extract) (the living
demons) (out of us) (we'd have to be very patient)

(so there'd be time to experiment) (rattle all
manner) (of exorcize-ese) (unholstered is their
lingo) (ready to fire is their jargon) (exclusive)
(society of ostracizers) (community of prohibitors)
(you have to undergo examination) (get background)
(checked) (promise to abide) (we abideth with one
another) (you are our promise) (we shoot you) (out)
(far) (into the future) (we'd been flares before)
(we'd been catapulted seeds) (so many times) (we

were used to it) (that is doubtful) (shady) (non-
sense detectable) (non-threadable) (the eye wouldn't
have it) (it was having none of it) (it couldn't
abide it) (there was no home for that) (watch of
nightingales) (too many nightlatches) (we were in
nightschool) (being schooled in all of the night-
time convergences) (it's no trick to get into that
school) (we could be nightwalking exclusively in one
another's company) (only yesterday) (out of range now)

sheetrock bizarre

(the hands) (on the clock were broken) (they
twitched back and forth) (saying very little)
(not telling) (keeping it to themselves) (nothing
could pry it out of them) (there was no crowbar)
(with enough leverage) (to get them to tell) (to
spill all) (that is hidden within them) (that is
knit-tight inside) (their brain switches) (their
that way and this do nothing breakers) (do any-
thing circuits) (crib switchers) (left and right

riders) (right and wrong throngs) (vector dis-
pensers) (tide watchers) (waterline markers)
(floodskids) (you can wash them off with peroxide)
(you can contemplate the froth) (they spew forth)
(we were almost) (we were just about) (we were
nearly) (we were close to) (drowning in a spoon-
ful) (of technicolor spectacles) (big blue shirts)
(green obscene scenery) (rocksolid obscurity) (not
in their faces) (their faces said everything)

(you think you're a boy now) (dressed up like a
soldier) (your rifle weighs close to nothing) (its
handle is hollow) (a good place to hide something)
(you are the sole soldier) (left to defend) (your
side) (may or may not be winning) (it's in the thick
of a battle) (so much smoke) (it's hard to see what
you are doing) (your canteen is empty) (you can hear
it thunk) (as you run) (from one hiding place to an-
other) (near a rockwall) (by a fallen treetrunk)

(in the cellars) (you turn into scientists) (you
admire many chemicals) (your friends are math
wizards) (periodical cicadas) (seventeen year
locusts) (they say there's been plagues of you)
(we darkened the sky) (we put the sun under)
(our noise drove them) (to open up their prayer-
books) (to see what we'd been sent for) (we'd
been sent in our perspicuous green iridescence)
(to build houses) (to spread ninepenny nails every-

where) (to employ hammers) (for something to saw for)
(for bricks to stack up to) (for trees to be skidways)
(for the invention of sheetrock) (to move gypsum
around) (worse comes to worst) (we can tear down the
walls) (they're pretty flimsy) (fists go through them
fairly easily) (fertilizer) (is what the walls are
made of) (in our crassitude) (we were entering into)
(horse latitudes) (you can follow the map of hyper-
bola) (you can rock to sleep in those waters) (you

can let your ship) (have its head now) (you can turn)
(off your engines) (turn out the lights in the pilot-
house) (drag your heavy blankets) (to the upperdecks)
(open your last tin of tobacco) (its lid had a compass
flower painted on it) (your rolling papers were see-
through) (they had great clarity) (there was no obstruc-
tion of vision) (we were far away from the centers of
power) (we couldn't find an official anything) (our
documents were drifting away from us) (they were

beautiful skimming the water's surface drifting
away documents) (identification icebergs) (our
tips were what we were known by) (there was more
attached to our tophats) (more time to be near)
(more ways to stand by) (more stars) (no other
lights) (just a few) (red embers) (that's how we
knew where to find you) (you were officially vagrant)
(vagabondage was your specialty) (you were its
captive) (they called you captain) (it was an

honorific) (and part of the honors of war) (to
let you leave) (with your flags flying) (to show
your little fence lizards) (were not incarcerated)
(for nothing) (they weren't skidproof) (we'd hit
the skids at that time) (we were broken crankshafts)
(our pharmacopoeia was looted) (we were into the
eighth day) (of the life of a nineday wonder) (but
we didn't know that) (we weren't fortune tellers)
(we didn't say) (I break my soul into pieces)

(we didn't say) (klaatus) (barada) (nikto) (and
into various persons) (we didn't say) (now for a while
no one will know you) (no one will say) (your name
when they see you) (they won't be saying) (I'll be
seeing you) (they won't do the how do you do) (you
can slip by) (without anyone) (noticing) (you will
have found a safe passage) (you can breathe easier)
(you don't have to look over your shoulders) (or keep
your eyes hidden) (you can look anyone straight in the eye now)

we wrote on wax tablets

(it wasn't watertight) (it never would be) (it
wasn't possible) (it's not in the cards) (that's
how we bent them) (for building what later we'd
watch fall down) (we were wrecking balls then)
(demolition experts) (there was great satisfaction)
(in arranging) (a pattern of circular rectangles)
(one inside the other) (to add to) (as many as we)
(could manage) (to get our hands on) (for building
long alleys and runways) (under the chairlegs)

(under the tables) (right up to the screendoor)
(then touch one) (and see if they'd form for us)
(a continuous falling) (forward) (without doing
damage) (the damage was already done) (we hadn't
smoothed) (down its feathers) (they were for)
(young birds) (came in boxes) (they came while)
(it was still winter) (they stayed near the fire)
(insanely peeping) (then nothing) (that caught
our attention) (we listened longer) (we were listen-

ing devices then) (ardent amplifiers) (then an
odd part of a beep) (could be heard coming from us)
(not a whole one) (once) (in a blue moon) (then
nothing) (silent as egg yolks) (as quiet as eyes)
(as unmoving marbles) (which we were losing) (no)
(something was putting them) (where we couldn't
see them) (into its pocket) (into a bucket) (tied
to a long rope) (that goes down a well shaft) (in
rapid descension) (we hit the walls while we were

going) (all the way to the bottom) (there was
cool air all around us) (we could hear water)
(saying) (what are you doing) (in my whereabouts)
(what are you coming with) (who sends you) (in my
direction) (what brings you) (to these questions)
(we have no answers) (we are just marbles) (rolling
around in a bucket) (we would have to) (put our
heads together) (and come up) (no) (we were down-
going) (remember) (how dark it was once) (we got

going) (the nearer) (we fell to the bottom) (with
something) (we wanted to say) (we are paying) (you
a visit) (it would be a pleasure) (to get to know
you) (we would have come sooner) (with something
to give you) (things to float on you) (things to
live in you) (some primeval ooze you might con-
sider) (some absinthe green slime) (for your ed-
ification) (we bring you) (what ails us) (was
our being) (out of your presence) (we wanted to

be near you) (water was silent) (it didn't say
anything) (it just stared at us) (as if we were)
(not speaking water) (we didn't know that language)
(we were unable) (to make ourselves clear) (this
barrier) (that was between us) (was going to have
to be acknowledged) (for it was a mighty strong
one) (we'd have to go around it) (over or under it)
(we were not breaking through it) (our atoms were
too close together) (walking through walls) (was

not an option) (it was standard equipment) (to
have many choices) (and scales) (I saw these fall
from your eyes) (upon which to weigh them) (in
order to glean) (they were gleaming) (barely a
hint) (gimme a hint they'd say to get closer)
(they'd say you're getting warm now) (they'd say
you're polar) (you're in frozen water) (better
hope you're a reptile) (we were clinking) (like
ice cubes) (clinking and peeping) (we were busy)

(going crazy) (they said they were all bi-polar)
(as if we had only two switches) (as if we couldn't
mingle) (we were very poor minglers) (as if we
had only two levers) (hot and cold running water)
(is luxurious) (we should have been furious) (fear-
less adventurers) (heading into the wilderness)
(arctic explorers) (artistic equivalents) (enduring
unbearable conditions) (getting low on provisions)
(our equipment was busted) (we had to change horses

too many times) (it was wearing us) (thin) (our spirits
were low now) (we had little morale) (it would take
a miracle) (I'm counting on you now) (I'm taking my-
self) (out of the picture) (it sounded as if) (there
was a grasshopper) (filing its nails) (the iron kind)
(inside the picture) (it was very peaceful) (it was
in a wheatfield) (after a harvest) (the family had
gathered) (in all their best outfits) (to stand and be
photographed) (to commemorate why they were sent here)

They have the following custom: when they know each other and see each other from time to time, before speaking they cry for half an hour.

(hope the gods never know who
you are) (pray they remain unknowing of your
existence) (go out of your way) (to escape
their notice) (if you see one) (about to catch
your eye) (look away) (flee) (for your life)
(if you see one coming) (duck into a doorway)
(duck into an alley) (hide behind a treetrunk)
(crawl under the covers) (hide in a closet)
(never) (if you can help it) (come to a god's

attention) (consider yourself) (fortunate if
you and the gods) (never cross paths) (try to
stay away from places they frequent) (they tend
to be attracted) (to some places) (bodies of
water) (mountain passes) (open country) (street
corners) (a shortcut you always take) (detours
you hazard upon) (a certain tree) (you always
notice) (they find you) (when you aren't thinking)
(about what they will do with you) (when un-

thinking of them) (is what you are doing)
(on a long walk late at night on a riverbank)
(standing with your face lit by a fire burning
in a barrel) (your unconscious staring into space)
(as you look up from a book) (and notice some-
thing) (attracts your attention) (sunlight some-
place you've never seen it before) (a pin stuck
straight up on a windowsill) (stray hair you find
on your shirt sleeve) (a ticking something electrical

is doing near by you) (a column of smoke
(is it smoke) coming out of an open window)
(low fog rolling onto a road) (a bend in a
river) (a curve of skin over a cheekbone be-
longing to someone you love) (this is a very
dangerous place) (we're on a collision) (course)
(chances are) (slim) (be the blade) (of grass)
(one of many) (blend in to the background) (little)
(impersonate) (a micron) (be a mite) (less

likely to notice you) (half a chance) (you
stand to) (see what it's like) (for them to
overlook you) (the parkbench overlooks a pond's
beach) (the advent of open water as you pass)
(out) (of a cypress grove) (overlooks) (prairie
grass beaten down in a hailstorm) (smashed)
(it will never stand again) (it's down) (for the
count) (there's no sun strong enough) (to pry
it back up again) (to pry it open) (to break into

it) (it's private) (as private as the dead)
(center of a planet's inner core) (you can't
get there from here) (there would be many fatal
detours) (you'd have no tread left) (your blade
would have worn down) (to nothing) (nothing could
sharpen it) (nothing could make it worse) (you'd
have to be melted) (you'd need to be molten)
(you wouldn't want to be) (yourself anymore)
(everyone you met) (just as before) (would meet

you as though) (you were a stranger) (standing
alone) (on a dock) (under a streetlight on a
deserted corner) (on a roadside out in the
middle of nowhere) (gods find these places)
(suit their fancy) (idle their curiosity)
(they go there prowling) (sniffing to find
something human) (because they can hurt it)
(then sit back and watch it) (there's no
deviation) (they are addicted) (to watching

us) (as we are) (to watching disasters) (glued)
(to a screen) (like we were melted down hoof
chips) (like we were moths trying to get into)
(where some light is) (someone left in a hurry)
(without turning the lights off) (they didn't
lock the door) (they left) (the windows wide
open) (they didn't close) (any of the shutters)
(they left) (the water dripping) (they left)
(their bags behind) (they were leaving) (they

left) (without saying a word) (they were good
leavers) (leaving is what they were good at)
(unsurpassed) (approaching perfection) (model
absquatulators) (ideal absentee) (landlords)
(we could live in their houses) (but we'd never
see them) (small chance) (we would know what to
say to them) (there would be nothing to say)
(we talk anyway) (talk about) (whose face you
saw) (floating in moonlit waters on a green lagoon)

spur reverie

(in this phase) (we traveled) (in the dark)
(in silence) (we communicated with our eyes)
(we couldn't see them) (we passed notes) (it
was too dark to read them) (we stayed in touch
with one another's backs) (we could hear trans-
ports flying by) (every five or ten minutes)
(it sounded as though they would turn off their
engines) (and pause) (long enough to deeply
inhale) (then move on) (in daylight they look

like great whales) (that've been kidnapped) (&
had giant wings fastened to them) (after every
thing whale about them) (has been taken away)
(freaks of nature) (that's us) (that's the slow
low flying whale-cum-plane) (despite what it was)
(we felt ambivalent about it) (we grew to depend
on them) (if we noticed their absence) (we'd
grow anxious) (we would start waiting for them)
(we couldn't sleep or rest) (their not being

where we were) (used to them) (their non-insistence)
(their no where) (to be found now) (their dis-
appearance) (we couldn't see) (where they had gone
to) (we couldn't follow them) (we weren't whales)
(we couldn't fly) (the more they were gone) (the
more we had them on our minds) (that's what they
say about) (absence) (proof of something's non-
existence) (it was as if we'd been abandoned) (it
was a new wound) (our nerves) (were raw) (it felt

as if we were grieving) (we weren't acheproof
then) (we were unprotected) (nobody's protégé)
(a solitary) (sorespot) (too very unwoeproofed)
(our woe was very) (underreported) (it was underrated)
(it was on-going undergoing) (it kept changing)
(so say the undersigned) (it was protean) (it was
piscine) (it was fishy) (we were pretty suspicious)
(of ourselves) (we were under selfsuspicion) (we
had no idea) (what our motives were) (up to) (now

we were motive-free) (we needed some spurs) (we
hadn't earned them) (we didn't know where the
proving grounds were) (at that time) (it seemed
as if they were everywhere) (in such great numbers)
(everywhere we looked) (coming at us) (left and
right) (it was raining) (cats and dogs) (we were
like kids) (in a rainstorm) (we didn't know what)
(drops we wanted) (we were outnumbered) (things we
needed) (we were numerously) (challenged) (what

might be) (good for us) (the place was teeming)
(what we might trust in) (the place was crawling)
(it was an out-and-out legions) (rout) (to whom
we should go to) (everyone was being tested) (under
whose protection) (under whose wing) (should we
find ourselves) (it was one thing) (to be tested)
(to see what we were made of) (something else al-
together) (to test us) (to see if we could be
frightened) (sufficiently enough) (so as to not

be able) (to ask our own questions) (about
their suspicious) (behavior) (suspicions of
us) (we were all suspects then) (they would
let us know) (what our motives) (were good for)
(their spurs were righteous) (it was their own
god-given spurs) (had been in their blood) (since
time began) (would be there) (by god) (til time)
(for all time) (til it stood still) (til hell)
(froze) (over and above us) (which wasn't likely)

(as it seems) (the place was getting all the more
warm (& fuzzy & cuddly & frilled & decoupaged &
decalled & denatured) by the minute) (it was enough)
(to turn your stomach) (we were getting a good)
(tongue) (whip) (lashing) (we might have to have)
(that x-rayed) (and wait for the results) (in a
waiting room) (in an unresolved situation) (they
call you back) (with a whistle) (you come when you
are called) (to listen) (to their speeches) (stop

everything) (you were doing) (to give them an
audience) (more than they give you) (so they can
hear themselves talking) (no one dare) (question)
(their motives) (saying they want) (to protect us)
(they want to protect) (the world) (as we know it)
(we will be better) (off) (in their protective) (cus-
tody) (we couldn't be trusted) (to know what was)
(good for us) (they were under (a delusion) a spell
of revenge reverie) (their spurs were silver, gold)

. . . The first have already disappeared.

(an edge of water was there) (crashing in)
(lapping onto) (bringing in) (taking out)
(leaving behind) (taking away) (worked on)
(because a moon was there) (and weathered)
(paths passed into this) (trails came by)
(a road was made) (salt went by) (soap came
along) (something weaved) (marks were made)
(something gave a repeatable noise) (someone
traced the shape of us) (in wet sand) (we

stood up) (to see what we were) (before the
next wave came) (and we were gone) (as if we'd
been sleeping) (it wasn't clear where we were)
(even as it dawned on us) (in bright daylight)
(or when the sun was gone) (as if our eyes were
adjusting) (to watching) (boats disappear)
(sails rising into view) (seeing one another's
faces in firelight) (watching one another) (to
see if anything was happening) (someone might

disappear) (or be gone a long time) (there
weren't so many of us) (one came by with a wheel)
(one with a song) (one dropped a seed in a hole)
(we crossed paths) (on the esplanade) (under the
circumstances) (in which we found ourselves) (we
needed to) (to find one another) (over and over) (or
else) (inertia) (quicksand) (inflexibility) (we
were bathing in lavabaths) (we were not inflammable
then) (it was a fairly stable suspension) (so

nothing was certain) (everything was) (up in
the air) (it was dangerous for birds) (we couldn't
say) (what might fall) (from the sky) (fish fell)
(frequently) (frogs fell) (a fire came by) (trees
blew away) (like they were toothpicks) (some of
them were toothpicks) (you presented me with a
newly forged pickaxe) (someone measured a rain-
fall) (someone figured out) (what diamonds were
good for) (lapis lazuli had a good run) (we carved

many things) (we were easily amazed) (we made up
labyrinths) (to keep our bulls in) (so we could
walk through) (how we were thinking) (to maximize
our confusions) (to have something to compare) (to
our poppyfields) (to give our cornfields) (mythical
status) (a lot had been settled) (and unsettled)
(revolts raised) (defeats replaced) (the end of this)
(death of that) (height of one thing) (decline of
another) (invasions) (reprisals) (reversals of

fortune) (someone put a sistrum in a baby's hand)
(up rose a new baby to conquer the world) (to dis-
pense with what had been before) (to improve things)
(so we could learn) (what progress means) (we were
spinning (things) too rapidly) (to keep up with them)
(to get them to look like we wanted them to) (we were
in a sorting machine) (we were no match for that)
(we were a handful of matches) (scattered over the
oceans) (we looked so peaceful) (from a perch on the

moon) (you know what they say) (about distance)
(it's distancing) (it gets under your skin) (in
increments) (like the way the seventh sense)
(and the ninth dimension) (are slowly coming into
being) (just beginning) (in the earliest stages)
(of evolution) (novasoma) (in any case) (their
development is under construction) (by the same
token) (the sad old gold bars no longer need to
be stored) (paper moon) (paper lanterns up and

down the levees) (your slow boat to China) (barely
raising a wake) (hypnotizing the shorebirds) (mes-
merizing the wharfrats) (destabilizing) (causing
bellbuoys to) (seem more mournful) (than usual)
(usually they seem) (beside themselves) (idly
aware of their whereabouts) (it's awful when they're
hysterical) (they sound as if they can't finish a
sentence) (they have too much responsibility) (com-
pletely at the mercy) (of their environment) (they

aren't organized) (they're moody) (they wear their
emotions on their sleeves) (which makes them very
straightforward) (if somewhat taxing) (they never
are not in motion) (even when it's barely percept-
ible) (they are ultra-sensitive motion detectors)
(birds land on them) (to amuse themselves) (to have
their brains rest awhile) (to leave civilization
behind) (it will be there) (when we return) (here
is where we were born) (why we wanted to return)

blood invention

(we made our beds on any porch we could find) (put
ourselves under) (sheets of mosquito netting) (we
looked as if we were waiting) (to be taken away)
(to the boneyard) (when anyone stumbled upon our
location) (we spooked them away) (we didn't betray
our disguises) (we weren't aroused when they shone their
lights on us) (it turned us into something for travelers
to find) (we were good motionless amulets) (we were
big cocoons) (we were going to be monumental swallow-

tails) (we'd be too big for flowers) (our shadows
would darken the landscape) (send children running)
(to hide under the tables) (they would look up) (from
what they were doing) (move without thinking) (to
look out from their windows) (their doors would open)
(to see where the day'd gone) (they'd put down their
ledgers) (their instruments would be still now) (they
wouldn't be doing now) (what they'd been doing before)
(sorting through their boxes) (arranging for things

to be taken) (away to) (shipping wouldn't be happening)
(they'd quit) (their calculations were in limbo) (the
ones in the fields) (with scythes and spades in their
hands) (would stop moving) (to see what we were doing)
(with our newly acquired iridescence) (no one would
recognize us now) (as we descended) (to congregate)
(to establish a parish) (along the banks of one of their
rivers) (it would have to be a mighty one) (we were
thirsty butterflies) (dry to the bone) (there were no

bones in us) (we were parched boneless wingspans)
(tired from our tireless) (we didn't have automobiles)
(fact-finding oscillations) (we studied woodgrain)
(in its infinite variations) (encoded in it) (were di-
rections) (maps we could follow) (we and woodgrain
were co-conscious now) (we shared our hallucinations)
(we understood one another's tongueslips) (we cured
one another's paragraphia) (part of the era's pandemic)
(we could dope out without twisting our heads off)

(unfamiliar) (remonstrance) (contra-remonstrance)
(surrebuttal) (fathomful parquetry) (we're sorry,
woodgrain) (soon there would be the advent of birds)
(an increase in land masses) (you are in a state of ex-
cellent kef now) (breathing as if you were one with
the paracletes) (nothing is moving) (your confetti
has been arrested) (that's where so many shredded
documents) (get second chances) (you patch them back
together) (they're stopped in mid-sentence) (we

may need a telescope to read them) (once we tape them
all back together) (we indicate that they are fragments)
(we make educated guesses) (and put words in their mouths)
(there are no mouths to put words in) (putting words in
mouths) (sounds almost disgusting) (is definitely sus-
pect) (they would dissolve there) (we would have lost
them) (we couldn't get to them fast enough) (we had slow-
going means of transportation) (our surrey with the
stealth on top was a sorry one) (sorry was stenciled)

(on all of our foreheads) (on the undersides of our
wingspans) (we were coming and going sorry dispensers)
(we were dispensation wranglers) (our sorries were
wild ones) (not easy to capture) (better off in the
wild) (zeniths) (cochineal was the color) (of dead
insects) (epics are slated to tell their stories)
(they're everywhere all over our windshields) (in our
caustic pomegranate bloodspatters) (tell that to the
woodgrain) (soon there would be an advent of forbear-

ance) (an increase in indulgences) (masses of newly
formed ultra-improved compassion bearers) (from zero-
zero they would come) (probably a little disoriented
in the beginning) (until their eyes adjusted) (pro-
bably a little weary at first) (we could lend them
our blanket drills) (we'd been sleeping) (or pretending
to be sleeping) (long enough) (probably fairly cautious)
(we can say to them) (they won't ever have heard it be-
fore) (where to throw their caution) (but it would be

misleading) (we'd just read the newspaper's caution a-
gainst overoptimism) (we should pass that along to them)
(these were really antiquated newspapers) (we'd found
them lining the cage of a parakeet) (a blue one) (then
a green one) (was the colors they came in) (they had
no flags) (no banners) (these hadn't yet been concocted)
(formula for scarlet dye) (was still in the works then)
(their fingers were still working over the patterns)
(ceaselessly working and working) (scarlet code crackers)

He drags the dead out of their coffins
and stands them again on their feet.

(more of you began to be circulating) (into focus)
(you could see yourself in different situations)
(surrounded) (you were still almost always the center)
(from which you looked out) (to try to find someone
you recognized) (who recognized you) (as a kindred)
(nerve center) (as allied) (spur-of-the-moment) (im-
provisions) (could be difficult to manage) (you
weren't managers of much) (you could barely) (manage
to be who you thought you might want to be) (minute

to minute) (your options were more than you'd ever
imagined) (all of a sudden) (you needed a haircut)
(on a particular day) (in a particular style) (that
would be certain) (to give you courage) (consequently
what you wore) (wore you) (out because it was constantly
changing) (and you could look back now) (enough time
had gone by) (there was room to remember) (you were not
the same then) (as you were getting to be now) (who
you were not all that long ago) (seemed remote) (seemed

altogether) (unrelated) (you could wince for who you
were) (you could feel a little pity) (a kind of nostalgia)
(you hadn't run into such an odd feeling) (formerly you
were one gear) (you had no reverse feelings) (to clash
with) (your surroundings were enlarging) (there were
going to be) (more and more layers of circumstances)
(repercussions) (and reverberations) (now and then)
(it gave you the look) (of a laminated headache) (you
arrived and departed simultaneously) (as if you epitomized)

(not knowing if you were coming or going) (managed
to keep those around you) (alerted) (you kept them
off guard) (you specialized in sudden repositioning)
(you were throwing your yokes off) (wrestling away
your splices) (launching yourself) (on unfamiliar ter-
rain) (in search of) (learning another language) (was
hidden inside your everyday one) (you would have to
learn how to find it) (it would take some trial and)
(plenty of error) (to shed from it) (its awkwardness

could turn you into a stranger) (version of yourself
than you'd bargained for) (a little trouble here &
there) (some physical damage) (it was necessary that
you establish a clear understanding) (with all of the
most basic elements) (you and fire had some things to
deal with) (there were chemicals) (that had to be
taken) (to your command station) (for interrogations)
(you were converting) (no longer unquestioning) (done
with asking) (why do you ask) (so many questions)

(we were in question central) (we were bartering) (trying)
(to trade) (to make trades) (we were in question bazaar
territory) (why do you ask) (you ask too many questions)
(if you ask me) (it was a time of terrible tangible
inquisitions) (some splitting of hairs) (tearing of
hair time) (some shifting) (some dodging) (very beautiful
evasions) (radiant secrets) (one day a whiff of a witch-
hunt) (one day a sweep of your whole neighborhood) (you
were getting into) (them-and-us-hood) (where many of

the questions wouldn't have to be asked) (they
were settled) (this was a more stable association)
(of like-minded occupants) (who'd recognized one
another) (as having much in common) (and so could
benefit) (from one another's presence) (and enter-
tain) (but not too often) (not necessarily directly)
(an entirely more to the point set of questions)
(severely truncated) (down to the essence) (the
ever alluring) (what's up) (question quintessence)

(you could ransack one another's minds with that one)
(which you did) (on a regular basis) (you were a
talkative people) (all of a sudden) (whispering or
saying or shouting) (for its own sake) (for the
sound effects) (to be uppermost) (these were highly)
(elaborate greeting ceremonies) (carefully circum-
scribed) (rituals of identification) (you could find
affirmation there) (things could be confirmed there)
(you are affirmed, my man) (you have landed in con-

firmation) (lay on the hands) (you have landed) (in
the lap of luxurious magnetic molecules) (everyone's
axis is shimmering) (to tantalize) (to be ceaseless
circulating instable conjunctions) (our red brethren
planet is closer to us) (than they are) (tonight than
it's been for close to 60,000 years) (there won't
be another time) (more years will have to go by)
(circumstantially different) (circles of least con-
fusion to look for) (galaxies of you) (to unleash)

x in fix

(reservations) (there were so many of them)
(revisions) (whatever suited their needs)
(provisions) (provided in abundance) (kept
hidden) (cables for the bridge) (airshafts
for the tunnels) (ambient air) (without a care
in the world) (all uncluttered) (footloose)
(hard to trace) (impossible to pin down) (on
the move) (in action) (without pity) (pin pity
down) (sore heart) (for such a long drawn out

sword) (writing's wordless heart beating) (pro-
mise) (virtually) (seamless) (like a coastline)
(very available) (there for the taking) (on prin-
ciple) (by hairline) (air hiding in there) (err
on the side of) (here in there) (ere we meet)
(ere in there) (find us here) (the in there)
(he in her) (her in here) (her in there) (ere
we go) (hat in hand) (knees down) (eyes aside)
(yes in eyes) (leading in pleading (ending in

lending)) (in descending) (order) (an air of con-
clusion) (to the proceedings) (something on the
order) (of a cushioned) (crash-landing) (an illu-
sion) (you're moving) (because you aren't) (your
train isn't) (scheduled for departure) (for another
twenty minutes) (went in twenty) (while a train)
(right outside your window) (is slowly leaving)
(you with the sensation) (o in you) (in in minutes)
(you are also leaving) (lo in slow) (motion in a

solution) (to a problem) (rain in train)
(you didn't see coming) (you hadn't been look-
ing) (in the right direction) (eyes misplaced)
(that's your best guess) (what were the odds)
(catalepsy in the casino) (resin resistance)
(a pad foot on casters) (is as in paisley)
(almost too) (intricate) (to follow the swifts)
(down into a chimney) (it's an ancient panto-
graph) (ere we equivocate) (we hesitate) (we

lose) (our bearings) (of good tidings) (fine
driftwood) (quiet shoreline) (mechanical shore-
birds) (print makers) (not one designee) (not
two) (not ten million) (bats under that bridge)
(ere we find paella) (resists jambalaya) (if it
needs to) (if that's what is) (needed) (to fix
what was broken) (and still is) (in need of so
many) (improvements) (come in increments) (almost
unnoticed) (we are too close to them) (to see

almost anything) (that hasn't been) (pointed out
to us) (retrospectively) (settled) (in for the
long haul) (you take the long view) (you were
born there) (you cut your teeth) (in that place)
(it gave you) (an accent) (some stressmarks)
(acute ones) (on the diagonal) (bias cut) (with
gore pleats) (to sway more) (gracefully) (ere
moonlight leaves) (the premises) (are many for
us) (to find one another) (not in another) (for

in former) (lifetimes) (ago) (we were feathers
then) (we were anthers) (we were pistols) (our
smoking guns) (were still smoking) (it was in)
(the time of long shadows) (we made wishes)
(on eyelashes) (our dna was still smoking) (it
had just been) (taken out) (of the fire) (we
stared into) (as if it would show us) (what we
were made of) (and where we had come from) (to
arrive) (at this juncture) (in these circumstances)

(under these conditions) (at this point) (in
time) (to keep an appointment) (ere an arrow
points in) (many directions) (around the hands)
(on a compass) (om is in there) (ass is) (row
is around) (round is how we go) (there's no way
around that) (it's a fixed bias) (and a bit)
(less awful) (than a straight line) (word stored
in sword) (we stored our provisions) (out of
reach) (of high tide) (away from pandemonium)

(demon in that one) (a very possessive one) (ere
we were demons for) (sticking together) (for the
most part) (we were) (inseparable) (per person)
(one at a time) (we shot back) (in reverse order)
(like swifts from a chimney) (to charm) (there's
no harm) (in there) (one another) (senseless)
(to stare) (at everything) (into one another's
eye secrets) (to see what they were saying) (ere
we close them) (ere flies an arrow out of time)

And prosper to the apoplex . . .

. . . Reverse we proved was not defeat . . .

. . . But, lagging after, who is . . .
Called early . . .

Acknowledgments

The author is grateful to the editors of: *The American Poetry Review, Crazyhorse, Denver Quarterly, Green Mountains Review, jubilat, The Massachusetts Review, The Melic, New American Writing, Octopus, Poetry Miscellany, Seattle Review, Turnrow,* and *Volt,* in which sections of this poem have appeared, sometimes in slightly variant versions.

x in fix appeared as #10 in *Rain Taxi's* Brainstorm Series.

With thanks to the Massachusetts Cultural Council for a fellowship which sustained some of this poem.

Epigraphs

Late 19th century epitaph, Emily Dickinson's tombstone engraving (13) / *Beowulf,* translated by Seamus Heaney (20) / Figure drawings by Guy Pettit, after *Arthur Gordon Pym* by Edgar Allan Poe (24) / James Merrill (32) / Edmund Spenser (38) / Arthur Rimbaud, translated by Wyatt Mason (46) / T.S. Eliot (50) / William Clark (54) / Wallace Stevens (62) / Christopher Smart (66) / William Carlos Williams (70) / John Ashbery (76) / Henri Michaux, translated by David Ball (82) / Jean Giorno, translated by Katherine Allen Clark (90) / Alain-Fournier (Henri-Alban Fournier), translated by Frank Davison (98) / Frank Stanford (104) / Xavier deMaistre, translated by Stephen Sartarelli (112) / Christopher Smart (116) / Cabeza de Vaca, translated by Martin A. Favata and Jose B. Fernandez (124) / Pierre Reverdy, translated by Lisa Beskin (130) / Walt Whitman (136) / Herman Melville (143)

DARA WIER, author of nine collections of poetry including *Hat on a Pond* and *Voyages in English* (Phi Beta Kappa Award Finalist), has received grants and awards from the Guggenheim Foundation, the National Endowment for the Arts, the Massachusetts Cultural Council, and *The American Poetry Review*. She teaches in the MFA program for poets and writers at the University of Massachusetts in Amherst.